D1171883

The Freedom of God

I will tell of the decree of the Lord:
He said to me, "You are my Son,
  today I have begotten you.
Ask of me,
  and I will make the nations your heritage,
and the ends of the earth your possession."
Psalm 2:7-8

"The philosophy of the Middle Ages rejected its task, which consisted in bringing to the world the idea, unknown to the ancients, of a created truth."
Lev Shestov, *Athens and Jerusalem*

The Freedom of God

A Study of Election and Pulpit

by

JAMES DAANE

WILLIAM B. EERDMANS PUBLISHING COMPANY
Grand Rapids, Michigan

Library of Congress Cataloging in Publication Data

Daane, James.
  The freedom of God.

  Includes bibliographical references.
  1. Election (Theology)   2. Preaching.
I. Title.
BT810.2.D32   252   72-77189
ISBN 0-8028-3421-3

TO JEAN

Contents

Introduction

Although I teach in a seminary, I am at heart a preacher —with an interest in theology. As a teacher of preaching I have been compelled to think about the theology of preaching. Often I have reflected on a question that cries for an answer: Why is election, which runs like a vertebra through the Scriptures, so rarely preached? This question is especially striking when asked within the Reformed theological tradition in which I stand. Election belongs to the hard core of Reformed theology: the theme of God's gracious election is a distinctive characteristic of Reformed theology. So the silence of Reformed pulpits on this theme is strange indeed.

When the sound of election is no longer heard in the pulpits of churches creedally committed to the truth of election, the situation would appear to warrant an investigation to discover whether the pulpit or the doctrine is at fault. This book is an effort to uncover the reason for this strange silence. There are two parts to the answer. One reason is that Reformed theologians have differed among themselves about election so profoundly that controversy has often deeply disturbed the churches. In reaction, for the sake of peace, there has been a tendency to mute the sound of election in the pulpit. Second, as the truth of God's election was refined more and more by influential Reformed theologians, election became increasingly unpreachable.

To trace the theological features and emphases that rendered election largely unpreachable is to become ever more aware that these had their roots in the decretal theology of seventeenth-century Protestant scholasticism. Reformed scholastic theologians like Francis Turretin constructed highly refined doctrines of a divine decree. This decree (often called "the plan of God") was regarded on the one hand as encompassing whatever comes to pass in all space and time, but on the other hand as bearing no *particular* relationship to what Paul designates as God's "intent," which, in Paul's words, is "according to the eternal purpose which he [God] has realized in Christ Jesus our Lord" (Eph. 3:11). Reformed decretal theologians generally theologized from a commonly accepted notion of an all-comprehensive divine decree that "accounts for all that happens in the world."

All thought that God's eternal purpose in Christ must be defined within the terms of God's all-inclusive decree; the biblically stated eternal divine purpose in Christ did not, in their thought, decisively determine the nature and purpose of God's decree. What God eternally purposed in Christ was left to be defined in the larger context of another more expansive decree. Whatever disagreements there were among these theologians occurred only within this basic commitment.

This book attempts to elucidate the differences between the scholastic view of God's decree and the biblical view of God's eternal purpose as decreed in Christ. We shall see how the scholastic version of God's decree governs most of the recent articulate proponents of Reformed theology and how this persistence of decretal theology accounts for the pervasive silence concerning the doctrine of election in Reformed pulpits. Although we shall be looking closely at the theological statements of some recent exponents of seventeenth-century decretal theology who demonstrate that such a doctrine of God's decree cannot be preached, our chief intent is positive, not critical. Our main concern is to demonstrate that God's only decree is the gracious and elective purpose that he in divine freedom purposed in Jesus Christ, and that this decree can be preached because it can be believed.

This book projects a view of God's decree understood as an act of his freedom in Jesus Christ. It is a view that differs significantly from the divine decree that scholastic theologians see as formulated outside of and antecedent to God's

purpose in Jesus Christ. The scholastic decree contains and
accounts for everything, including sin. The decree of God's
purpose in Christ does not account for sin but savingly
triumphs over it.

The problem this book addresses is large, deep, and complex, but its size, depth, and complexity arise in the main
from the way decretal scholastic theology defined election. I
am certain that I have not probed all the biblical heights and
depths of election, nor achieved a theologically inerrant reflection of the Bible's teaching about election. A genuinely
Reformed theology is never a final theology: like the church,
it is constantly summoned to reform itself in the light of the
demands of Scripture. So this book makes no pretense to
theological finality. But it has been written and published in
the conviction that it opens a window on a clearer biblical
view of election than that offered by decretal theology, a
view that can help return election to the pulpit. Without this
confidence, it would not have been written.

But books do not emerge out of mere confidence. This
book was made possible by a quarterly sabbatical graciously
given by Fuller Theological Seminary, and by the encourag-
ing insistence of the late Calvin P. Bulthuis, Vice President of
Eerdmans Publishing Company, for many years Managing
Editor of the *Reformed Journal,* and long-time personal
friend.

James Daane

Altadena, California

CHAPTER I

The Sum and Substance of the Gospel

The first sermon in the history of the Christian church was preached by the apostle Peter on Pentecost, the day the New Testament church was born. What was the topic of that sermon? God's election of Jesus, the core of Christian truth.

Peter rebuked the house of Israel for rejecting Jesus of Nazareth, a man whom God had approved of in many ways, and for crucifying him through the hands of lawless men (Gentiles). But Peter does not stop with accusation. The good news is that he whom Israel rejected is God's elect. God raised him from the dead. Peter recapitulates his entire sermon in the conclusion: "Let all the house of Israel therefore know assuredly that God has made him both Lord and Christ, this Jesus whom you crucified" (Acts 2:36).

The effect of Peter's sermon on man's rejection and God's election of Jesus was powerful. Convicted of their sin, men cried out, "Brethren, what shall we do?" Peter's response was "repent and be baptized." Repent of your sin of rejection, and be baptized into him whom God has chosen to be the Christ.

This double demand corresponded to the two parts of Peter's sermon, which corresponded in turn to the two central Christian events: the cross and resurrection. Both events have to do with Jesus' election. The cross occurred because men rejected Jesus' claim to be God's elect. The resurrection was God's demonstration of Jesus' status as God's elect.

If we listen to what was said, according to the four Gospel

9

writers, at the foot of the cross, we hear only one subject. All
the conversation and mockery turned on the issue of Jesus'
election. The Romans ridiculed Jesus only within the limits
of their understanding of the cross. As did Pilate, the Roman
governor, in his superscription, the Roman soldiers mocked
only Jesus' claim to be the king of the Jews. But every bit of
recorded Jewish discourse at the cross concerned Jesus' election. His claim to be the chosen of God was the target of all
their scorn. If indeed the Jews at the cross talked of anything
else, none of the Gospel writers thought it significant enough
to record. This is surely not without relevance, since the
Evangelists were guided by the same Spirit who gave the
church its voice on the day of Pentecost.

The Jews knew what was at issue at the cross. They
rejected Jesus' claim to divine election. So during his crucifixion, they directed their burning derision at this claim. Men do
not ordinarily laugh at a suffering, dying man. But here
election was the issue, and the Jews knew it. Luke tells us
that the people stood by watching, but the rulers scoffed:
"He saved others; let him save himself, if he is the Christ of
God, his chosen One." The other Gospel writers tell us that
"the chief priests," "the scribes," and "the elders" hurled the
same shafts of mockery: if you are the Christ, the King of
Israel, the son of God (all variant ways to express God's
election of Jesus), save yourself, come down from the cross
and we will believe your claim to be all of these things as
God's elect.

There was a note of triumph to the mockery of the Jews at
Calvary. They construed their success in bringing Jesus to the
cross as a demonstration that they were right and Jesus
wrong, and they found a proof text in the Scriptures. According to Deuteronomy 21:23, any man who hangs on a
tree is accursed of God. Jesus' presence on the cross meant
that he was not God's Christ, not God's chosen one, but
someone rejected and cursed by God.

Against that background, Peter's sermon topic on Pentecost was not a random choice, something he happened to
have on his heart that he decided to share with his hearers.
No, Peter preached on the only thing he could have preached,

the subject that lies at the heart of the cross and the resurrection—God's election of Jesus. This continued to be the heart of Peter's preaching. Its theme according to Acts 3 and 4 (and Peter's first epistle) is: "This is the stone which was rejected by you builders, but which has become the head of the corner" (Acts 4:11). The same theme informs Paul's determination to know nothing else but Jesus Christ, that is, Jesus as God's "Chosen One," and him crucified.

If the scriptural curse on everyone who hangs on a tree is true, and if the cry of dereliction, "My God, my God, why hast thou forsaken me?" is given its full force, then the disclosure that God's curse and rejection of Jesus does not exclude Jesus' being the elect of God must be a shattering event, which does more than disclose what was always and timelessly true. And the resurrection is such an event. It is no mere demonstration or sign of what is, quite apart from itself, real and true. The resurrection *was* God's elective act, the act that constituted his election of the man, Jesus of Nazareth. As Peter said in his Pentecost sermon, God "made" him to be both Lord and Christ. This occurred at the resurrection. The election of Jesus is no abstract, timeless, non-historical truth, which the resurrection simply revealed as an eternal truth heretofore concealed. Jesus had to *become* God's elect; and by the resurrection God made Jesus of Nazareth Lord and Christ, his chosen one. We shall discuss this more fully later; for the moment, it is enough to recognize that Peter's sermon, with its double demand to repent and be baptized, concerned the election of Jesus as it related to the cross and to the resurrection.

Because the event of the resurrection can no more be dissociated from the living Christ than it can be from the election of Christ, the event *apart from Christ* reveals neither Christ's resurrection nor his election. Hence when the men of Emmaus left Jerusalem for home, dejected by the crucifixion, which had blasted all their hopes, they said, "We had hoped that he was the one" (Luke 24:21). The amazing report of some women that the tomb was empty was not enough. The men of Emmaus read the cross as the Jews had: everyone who hangs on a tree is cursed. The cross meant that

Jesus was rejected by God. And these two men came to know that "he was the one" only when the living Christ disclosed his identity in "the breaking of the bread."

Saul of Tarsus, later to become the greatest theologian and missionary the church ever had, the man who wrote more about election than any other biblical writer, also knew that the issue at the cross was election. Himself a Jew, he shared the Jewish understanding of the cross as proof of God's rejection of Jesus. Saul had played no role in the crucifixion, but when his time came, he acted on his theology of the cross with animus and vigor. He persecuted the church. He began by playing a minor role in the execution of Stephen. When Stephen preached to the Jews in Jerusalem that the one whom they had "betrayed and murdered" was God's elect, his hearers become violent and intent on stoning him to death. Saul consented to this execution: to make it easier for those who hurled the stones, he held their garments.

Consent soon developed into spirited aggression. Saul's theology of the cross demanded forceful action. If God had rejected Jesus, no one must believe—let alone preach—that Jesus was accepted by God. In this conviction he persecuted the church, first in Jerusalem, where he "laid waste the church . . . entering house after house" (Acts 8:3). Even this was not enough. "Still breathing threats and murder" (Acts 9:1), he obtained permission from the high priest to persecute the church in Damascus. On the road from Jerusalem to Damascus, Saul was struck down by a bright light and arrested by a voice he could not identify. The voice cries, "Why do you persecute me?" Saul responds, "Who are you, Lord?" The answer comes back out of the heavenly light and glory, "I am Jesus." In one flashing moment of insight, Saul is compelled to change his mind completely about Jesus. His earlier estimate is wholly reversed. He whom Saul had thought accursed of God is alive, standing at God's right hand. God had indeed rejected Jesus, but out of the death of rejection had raised Jesus as his elect.

With this recognition of the election of Jesus, Saul is converted. His recognition of the living Jesus as God's elect and his own experience of conversion form a single unit of experience. Within the knowledge of Jesus' election, Saul

becomes Paul, knows his own election, and receives his task
to be God's "chosen instrument" to "Gentiles and kings and
the sons of Israel" (Acts 9:15) by bearing the Lord's name.

All the component parts stand related like a cone of
concentric circles. Out of the basic knowledge of God's
election of Jesus arise Paul's knowledge of his own election,
his knowledge of his peculiar task as a chosen instrument for
Gentiles and Jews, and his knowledge of the peculiar mystery
of the church. To isolate any of these elements is to destroy
Pauline theology.

Karl Barth was correct when he said that election is the
sum and substance of the gospel, and that at the heart of the
gospel stands Jesus as God's elect.

CHAPTER II

The Gap Between Election and Preaching

Sermons on election are so rare that even a regular church-goer may never hear one. Through the years I have asked many church people when they last heard a sermon on election, and with rare exceptions most answered that they could not recall. Many believed that they had never heard one. And the rare occasion when a minister does venture to preach on election is more likely to be an apologetic lecture defending a particular form of the doctrine than a sermon proposing election as something in which the hearer should place his faith and ground his trust.

Even the faithful attender of almost any church, then, would never surmise that election runs like a vertebra through Old and New Testament alike. He may know that the burden of the Old Testament is the history of a "chosen people," but he seldom, if ever, hears a sermon on the divine election that conferred on Israel its special status and destiny. And the man in the pew may not even know (because he never heard it from the pulpit) that Jesus Christ and the church are objects of God's election. Nor would he be likely to surmise that election has been a major item on the agenda of most of the greatest theologians of the church and has played a very formidable role in shaping the church's diverse theological traditions. No other doctrine has been so decisive in theology and so ignored in the pulpit.

This gap between election and preaching exists in both Reformed and non-Reformed churches. It is especially remarkable in the Reformed churches, for election has played a large role in the Calvinistic tradition. And our intent in this book is to discover why such a formidable doctrine receives scarcely an echo in Reformed pulpits. But before we look at that question we should note that election is also a rare subject in the pulpits of the non-Calvinistic churches of the Reformation. These churches generally embrace a version of the nature of God's election that is characterized as "Arminian." Although there is no single, uniform "Arminian" doctrine of election, all the varied Arminian constructions of election have a common element that clashes with the distinctive feature of the Reformed doctrine of election.

*   *   *

In the Reformed doctrine of election, God's elective action is *decisive*. It is God's act alone, not contingent on human action, not based on foreseen human cooperation and faith. Nor is election something that can be undone by human unbelief. Election is that decisive act by which God determines that he in all the fulness of his life will be the future of man. A full definition of election would of course include much more than this statement; but here it is sufficient to point to the decisive character of God's elective action, for it is at this point that all Arminian versions diverge from the Reformed doctrine.

All Arminian versions of election in the non-Reformed Protestant churches (theologically, the Roman Catholic Church can also be included here) hold that the sinner retains the right and the ability, against every overture of divine election and grace, decisively to reject God's elective choice. This is regarded as authentic freedom. Man's choice is ultimately decisive. God's grace never violates man's freedom or right to say No to God. If God by a gracious elective action deprived sinful man of his freedom to say No, then God (it is said) would be in violation of man's freedom. The sinner is never so overwhelmed by the elective love and grace of God that he can only surrender to it. On the contrary, the sinner's authentic freedom remains impregnable to God's elective love; it retains the power and right of self-determination—to choose God as his future, or to choose a future without God.

This is a strange kind of "authentic freedom." The sinner is regarded as having freedom from God to reject God, yet not having freedom to escape the eternal consequences if he exercises that freedom and does reject God. It is a freedom that sounds like the stereotyped Soviet election—one is free to vote against the Party—and then to go to prison. In Arminian theology, the sinner is not obligated, but merely invited to be saved. But it is an invitation to heaven that sends him to hell if he declines.

One sees nothing of the invitational in the biblical account of the Lord's confrontation of Saul on the Damascus road, nothing of an "authentic freedom" to say No in the account of Paul's conversion. As Karl Barth has observed, election in biblical thought is God's election of man, not man's election of God. But election in Arminian theology is a description of the possibilities of human freedom. In theological idiom, that kind of election falls within natural theology. For although some would regard this freedom to choose or reject God as a gift of "enabling grace," it in fact characterizes the nature of man who has not yet become a Christian. It is as a natural, non-Christian man that man possesses and exercises the freedom to choose or reject God.

What distinguishes natural theology from revealed theology is that the former points to what is true about man before he becomes a Christian. For this reason the truths of natural theology are not the content of preaching. No form of enabling grace (including common grace) can be preached—that is, proclaimed as something to be believed by faith—since such forms of grace are by definition something the non-Christian already possesses. So they are not part of the good *news*. The content of natural theology can be no more than something to be used to further revealed theology, apologetic leverage for the acceptance of the gospel, if you will. The truths of natural theology about natural man can be prolegomena to the gospel, but natural theology is not a part of the gospel, an element of the content of preaching.

Thus we see why election is not preached in churches whose doctrine of election is in the Arminian tradition. The Arminian doctrine of election as a possibility of human freedom cannot be preached, for to do so would be to preach man, not Christ, and the Arminians have no desire to preach anything more or less than Christ and him crucified.

But although Arminians do not and cannot *preach* their particular doctrine of election, they do *use* it. And their use of it corresponds precisely to their understanding of it as a possibility of the sinner's authentic freedom. They use it *after* the sermon, in the appeal to the sinner to exercise his freedom and make a "decision for Christ," and thus as something that is not an integral part of their proclamation. Election comes into play at the altar call, when the summons is issued for acceptance of what was heard. The Arminian preaches the word of God, and then *adds* something: a human appeal to the sinner to exercise his freedom by deciding for Christ. This appeal is *added* to the sermon because the Arminian believes that the word itself does not have the inherent right and power to bring the sinner to a surrender to God unless his freedom grants prior consent.

So this Arminian view of election is open to the protest that it turns God's election into a human act. But it also invites the objection that the inner sanctuary of freedom that Arminian theology concedes to the sinner and does not allow the elective power of God to enter is—often by a calculated entree—invaded by the Arminian preacher of the gospel. The very freedom that Arminian theology concedes to the sinner, the Arminian preacher violates. This disparity between theology and practice is most apparent where the preacher regards himself as an evangelist. No preacher more resorts to "ways and means," emotive strategies, fear, sentiment, gimmicks, publicity, and organization than the preacher of an Arminian gospel. Confronted by a sinner whom he regards as ensconced within the impregnable walls of his authentic freedom to reject God, the Arminian preacher, unarmed by a gospel of elective power able and permitted to enter that sanctuary, is caught in a contradiction. Either he does not preach the gospel to sinners at all, or he invades and thereby violates their freedom in an effort to induce them to accept the gospel.

In the light of this, it follows that the more a church's theology is dominated by Arminianism, the more that church will resort to finding ways and means of influencing sinners, and the less faith it will have in its public preaching services and ministry of prayer. In many evangelical church services more time and greater zeal is devoted to the post-sermon appeal to unbelievers than to prayer to God.

The degree of imposition and manipulation of the sinner's freedom may at times be minimal, but this is determined more by the personal preferences of the preacher than by theological considerations. But the inherent nature of the Arminian view of election is an open invitation to invasion. And justification for such invasion in the name of seeking what the preacher regards as the sinner's highest spiritual interest is, for all its good intentions, indistinguishable from the justification offered by the exponents of slavery and other forms of human tyranny who often argue that they must violate a man's freedom for his greater good.

More significant than this is the observation that the Arminian, by his after-the-sermon efforts to induce the sinner to make the right choice and decide for Christ, demonstrates that the Arminian doctrine of election *is not preachable*. The absence of election in the Arminian sermon comports with the nature of Arminianism's theological understanding of election. Arminianism cannot preach election because it does not regard election as an act of God and, therefore, as an action of his Word; election is merely a possible response the sinner may make to the Word.

*   *   *

We have seen that churches committed to Arminian theology cannot preach election. So it would be incorrect to say that in these non-Reformed churches there is a gap between election and pulpit. There is surely, however, a gap between election and pulpit in Reformed churches. Election is little more preached in Reformed pulpits than in Arminian pulpits. But Reformed theology requires the preaching of election as an act of God—and a decisive one. Election must find a place in the sermon because the word of the sermon has as much power and right to invade the sinner's inner sanction of freedom with the freedom of God's election, as it has to punish the sinner for his wrong choice. The testimony of

Calvin, the Canons of Dort, and the Westminster Confession agree on this. Yet Reformed pulpits rarely comply. What is confessed in creed is scarcely preached in pulpit.

But the gap between the Reformed doctrine of election and the Reformed pulpit is much more serious. Not only is election scarcely whispered in most Reformed pulpits, but the Reformed doctrine of election has at times imperiled the very possibility of preaching the gospel. If Arminianism (which is shorthand for a peculiar definition of election) was unable to include election *within* its preaching of the gospel, Reformed theology (which is shorthand for another definition of election) was at some points in its history theoretically unable, because of its view of election, to preach the gospel at all. To this history we shall now turn.

In classical Reformed theology, election does not stand alone. Although Scripture speaks of predestination to life and never, explicitly, of predestination to damnation, election in Reformed thought implies its opposite, reprobation. Election was regarded as selection, a divine choice by which some men were predestined to eternal life, and all other men were regarded as reprobates predestined to eternal damnation. With election, reprobation emerges. This dual aspect was frequently called "double predestination."

The combination of election and reprobation created considerable intellectual difficulties for theologians, as the long history of Christian thought reveals. But for those called to preach the gospel, it created an even greater practical problem. How could one preach election?

The difficulty here stems not from election, but from reprobation. If all men were elect, the preaching of election would create no problems. One could preach election as he preaches all other Christian truth: by proclaiming it and calling people to believe it. But since some men are reprobates, the elect are not known. And if they cannot be identified from the vantage point of the preacher of the gospel, how can election be preached, even to the elect?

This is the apparent peculiarity of the doctrine of election. Every other Christian doctrine is susceptible to proclamation. None contains an inherent difficulty for the preacher. All can be projected in preaching; all can be proffered as truth that men ought to believe. But it is not so with the doctrine of election. It is true only of the elect, and there is nothing in the act of preaching that makes them identifiable. This is not to say that God's elect people cannot be known. It is only to say—and for the pulpit this is much—that there is nothing *in the act of preaching* that makes the elect identifiable to the preacher. Election indeed lends itself to lectures and theological reflection, but it appears impossible to preach—except to those identified as elect by some method that preaching itself does not possess.

But, one might argue, the solution seems easy enough. If election logically implies reprobation—if each is one face of the same coin—then any preaching of election is also, by logical implication, a preaching of reprobation. An explicit sermon on election is an implicit sermon on reprobation. Why not preach both—election explicitly and reprobation implicitly? But reprobation is not something that can be preached at all. The content of Christian preaching is something in which men are summoned to believe and trust to the saving of their souls. Reprobation does not satisfy that criterion. Reprobation is ultimate judgment—and no man can hope, trust, and have faith in that. The Bible indeed speaks of judgment, and the pulpit must proclaim judgment, but the Bible does not teach and the pulpit cannot preach an irreversible ultimate judgment *as an object of faith.*

Moreover, a further complication arises from the assertion of prominent Reformed theologians that no man has a right to believe that he is a reprobate. Herman Bavinck, one of the great theologians of the Reformed tradition, contended that every man receives such an abundance of God's blessings that he has no right to believe himself reprobate.[1] Calvin agrees with Augustine that in our preaching of predestination we must "be so minded as to wish that all men be saved."[2]

Now if Bavinck is correct in saying that every man experiences so many evidences of God's blessings that he is not allowed to think of himself as reprobate; if Calvin is right

---

[1] Bavinck says not only that no one may believe himself reprobate, but also that no one can, and no one actually does believe himself reprobate. *Gereformeerde Dogmatiek*, I, 422.

[2] *Institutes*, III, xxiii, 14.

that the church must preach with an attitude of wishing all men to be saved and thus must not regard any man as reprobate; if reprobation is not a proper object of faith and trust, then reprobation is indeed a most unusual Christian doctrine. And in view of this, it is remarkable that Reformed churches should include in their official, public, creedal confessions of faith a doctrine they cannot preach "to all nations" and to "every creature" (though they may attempt to "preach" it to the *elect*), a doctrine they believe no man may apply to himself. Clearly, reprobation as something implicit in election as its logical other face makes election itself difficult to preach.

Given all these inherent difficulties, it is not surprising that the sound of election has been muted in Reformed pulpits.

*   *   *

But the Reformed doctrine of election has not only tended to mute its own sound in the pulpit, it has at times even imperiled the possibility of preaching the gospel. The Reformed churches were aware of the so-called Great Commission and wanted to be faithful to their obligation to preach the gospel to all nations (Matt. 28:19) and to every creature (Mark 16:15). But in the attempt to be faithful to the truth of election, Reformed thought tried to understand the gospel in terms of election and in the process sometimes nearly lost the gospel by rendering it unpreachable.

In the process of understanding and defining the gospel by reference to election, such Reformed formulations emerged as the secret divine will in distinction from the revealed will of God, limited atonement, common grace in distinction from special grace, the internal and external covenant, and the covenant as a legal datum and as a datum of life-and-fellowship. To analyze all these theological formulations would move us into the wider context of this discussion; it is enough here to point out that while these theological constructions engendered considerable theological controversy, often creating unrest and sometimes causing ecclesiastical divisions, none of these matters can really be regarded as an authentic part of the pulpit's message. All these cited matters shape preaching, but are not themselves preachable. During the times they were in the center of controversy, they did find their way into the pulpit; but once the controversy was over, their sounds were no longer heard in the pulpit. The instinct of the pulpit triumphed over the emotions of the controversy.

We should, however, take a closer look at how election threatened the very possibility of preaching the gospel. If election means that the gospel is good news only for the elect, how can it be preached in that distinctive and authentic manner which distinguishes preaching from mere lecturing? This question arose in Scotland in the seventeenth century. Eminent Scottish Reformed theologians contended that the doctrine of election precluded the preaching of a gospel offer of salvation to all men. Some of these theologians held to an indiscriminate offer of salvation—but only to the membership of the visible church. This localized the problem, but did not solve it. Left unanswered was the question how a church loyal to the truth of election could preach the gospel to the world outside the church.

During the eighteenth century the same problem arose in the Reformed churches of the Netherlands. Election again challenged the addressability of the gospel to all men. One side in this Dutch controversy contended that the gospel as the good news of salvation could be preached only to men whose lives gave evidence of an operation of divine grace. Only these could safely be regarded as numbered among the elect, and the good news of salvation was for the elect only. Thus identification of the elect became an indispensable condition for proper proclamation of the gospel. A person's election had to be established *to the satisfaction of the judgment of others,* and established *apart from the gospel,* before his eligibility to hear the good news could be determined. Until the trustees of the gospel were satisfied that he was elect, it was not permissible for them to proclaim and for him to hear and believe that the gospel was good news for him. Curiously, this identification of a hearer as elect before he heard the gospel and without aid from it was not regarded as something forbidden by the warning against "vainly at-

tempting to investigate the secret ways of the Most High"
(Canons of Dort, I, 14).

On the other side of the controversy were those who
recognized this position as theologically absurd and religiously impossible. They contended that the nature of the
gospel is such that it can and must be preached as the good
news of salvation to all men. It is interesting—and theologically significant—that the theologians on this side of the
controversy were dubbed "new lights," that is, liberal theologians bringing a new, strange light to fall upon the relation
of election and preaching. And the theologians who opposed
these "new lights" and muted preaching in the name of
election by making identification of the elect an indispensable condition for the addressability of the gospel were
designated as "old lights," that is, conservative theologians
faithful and loyal to the Reformed tradition.

Notice that in both these controversies the central question was not whether or how *election* could be preached, but
whether election, as it was understood, allowed the *gospel*
itself to be preached. When the conservative element conceded that the gospel could be preached, but only to the
"visible church," or only to persons who could indicate their
eligibility by demonstrating their election, they did not demonstrate that their position had biblical sanction. How could
they? They had filtered the gospel through their doctrine of
election and thereby created the problem. And they could
appeal to nothing in the gospel to support their position
because the gospel in the biblical record nowhere describes
itself as good news only for the elect. On the contrary, the
Scriptures contend that the gospel must be preached to every
man. These "old light" conservatives offered only a compromise that neither Scripture nor their theology sanctioned.
Membership in the visible church is no guarantee of election,
nor is the ability of any person to convince others that he is
elected by God and therefore has the necessary credentials to
hear the gospel. The self-styled conservatives in both Scotland and the Netherlands recognized a contradiction between
the gospel and their doctrine of election. What they offered
was only a compromise, not a solution, and their compromise

was a compromising of the gospel, not an amendment of
their view of election.

                    *   *   *

Neither seventeenth-century Scottish, nor eighteenth-century Dutch theologians succeeded in bridging the gap between election and preaching. The gap continued into the
twentieth century, when new and ingenious proposals were
made to bridge it. Let us now look at some of these.

Herman Hoeksema, the leading churchman and theologian
of the Protestant Reformed Churches, regarded the doctrine
of election and reprobation as the distinctive feature of the
Reformed faith. His interpretation of the gospel in terms of
election and reprobation had never before been offered in the
history of the church. Hoeksema himself insisted that the
theology he developed was simply sound Reformed theology,
rooted in the Reformation and the Reformed creeds—in
particular in the Canons of Dort—but one of his colleagues
paid him the tribute—at his funeral—of saying that he carried
Reformed theology forward.

The distinctive features of Hoeksema's theology, which
arose from his interpretation of the gospel in terms of election and reprobation, are indicated in the following brief
statements: God loves the elect because they are righteous in
Christ; he hates the reprobate because they are sinners. The
elect alone are the object of grace; for them alone the gospel
is good news. For the reprobate God has no blessing at all,
but only an eternal hatred. Rain and sunshine, the hearing of
the gospel, the sacrament of baptism (if administered to a
person as an infant)—all are curses heaped on the reprobate.
The gospel is never an offer of salvation—neither to the elect
nor to the reprobate.

Here it is necessary to consider only Hoeksema's rejection
of the idea that the gospel is an offer of salvation. The
preaching of the gospel, he urged, does not *offer,* but *actualizes,* the salvation of the elect—and no less the damnation of
the reprobate. Thus the gospel is defined in terms of a divine
power that accomplishes God's sovereign purpose to save
elect men and to damn reprobate men. It must be admitted

at this point that the term "offer" is an idiom more suitable to Arminian theology than Reformed, for its connotation is one of God issuing an invitation and then waiting for men to accept it. The gospel as "offer" is apt for those who believe that man as free always retains the right to reject the gospel. This difficulty can be solved only if it is clear that terms like "offer" and "invitation to salvation" are of a peculiar kind in this context. The *offer* of the gospel is not optional, and the invitation to salvation does not have an RSVP. For judgment follows a rejection. Thus neither term should be regarded as a neutral term corresponding to that neutral freedom which Arminianism grants the sinner.

Hoeksema also rejected the concept of offer because it was regarded as a well-meant offer. He argued that God has no well-meant intentions toward the reprobate, only toward the elect. Furthermore, an offer bespeaks a *condition* that, when fulfilled by man, God *responds to.* Hoeksema emphasized that God is sovereign, and he took divine sovereignty to mean that nothing God does is a *response* to what man has done. God is never conditioned by man. Man's actions cannot become conditions for God's responses. God's judgments and his acts of reprobation are not a response to man's sin. God as sovereign determines and accomplishes whatever comes to pass. Hence Hoeksema contends that in the preaching of the gospel God makes no offers to man, presents no conditions for human acceptance and fulfilment. Rather, through proclamation, God actualizes the salvation of the elect and the damnation of the reprobate, without any responsive reference to the situations and conditions created by human action. So when Hoeksema rejected the idea of an offer and the notion of condition inherent in it, he was not merely protecting Reformed theology against Arminianism, but he was also protecting his own theological conviction that God as sovereign never acts—either in salvation or judgment—in response to something done by man.

Hoeksema understood both election and reprobation as sovereign divine acts that are in no sense a divine response of mercy or justice to fallen, sinful, and death-ridden men. Mercy does not cast an explanatory light upon election, for mercy thus understood would be a divine response to sinful man's misery. Hoeksema does not deny that God is merciful. But to avoid saying that mercy is God's response to man's self-effected situation of misery, Hoeksema maintains that God-in-himself is merciful, that is, that God is merciful to himself. Hence when God shows mercy to sinful man, mercy cannot be regarded as something *new*, as a divine *response* to man's lost condition.

Similarly, Hoeksema contends that God's grace for the elect sinner is not a form of divine love freely assumed in response to man's sinful plight. Grace is not a response to the human condition. Grace exists in God as he is in himself. God, says Hoeksema, has grace for and toward himself. Thus grace for the sinner does not emerge as something *new*, as a divine *response* to something outside of God.

Again, Hoeksema contends that when God speaks to man, he speaks not so much to man as to himself. God's word spoken in Christ is less spoken to man than to himself.[3] If God spoke to man redemptively in Jesus Christ, God would be responding to a condition lying outside of himself. Finally, Hoeksema contends that when God loves man, his love is not at bottom a response to the reality of man but to himself, for in loving man God loves only his own image in man, and thus his love for man is primarily an act of self-love.[4]

Hoeksema and those who followed his theology in the Protestant Reformed Churches preached election and reprobation. But is such preaching a proclamation of the gospel? Hardly. First of all, nothing about such a gospel is new. But the gospel as good news *is* something new and *proclaims* something new. In order to maintain an eternal, uncondi-

---

[3] Hoeksema, *Reformed Dogmatics*, pp. 16-17.

[4] If any divine *responsive* action is seen as a conditional action, and if it is rejected on that account, what meaning is left to God's judgment on sin and his wrath against the sinner? Hoeksema replies by eternalizing the wrath of God. In order to do that, divine wrath must be seen as internalized within God, with the result that it is seen as an attribute of God *apart from any external object of wrath*. Such a God is *in himself* a God of wrath. What is rejected here is far more than the conditionality found in Arminianism. Conditionality as defined and rejected by decretal theology is an overkill of Arminian theology, an overkill that exacts its price within decretal theology. Cf. Hoeksema, *Reformed Dogmatics*, pp. 104-123.

tional election and reprobation, Hoeksema is driven to define God's grace and mercy and his speech in Christ to man as realities that exist within God apart from any relation to man. The expression of grace and the like to man is really, Hoeksema says, an expression of God's eternal grace and the like *to himself.* There is nothing *new* about such a gospel. Its truth was not shaped as a response to man in sin and death; its truth always was. The gospel has no inherent connection with history, no peculiar nexus with man the sinner. In history it is merely made known. In short, it does not truly and distinctively speak to sinful man's condition and need, because it eternally speaks primarily to God's condition, that is, to a condition free of sin and death.

In the second place, the gospel understood thus has lost its meaning. What is primarily good news for a sinless and deathless God cannot be understood as good news for sinful, death-ridden men. What indeed is the meaning of divine grace? of mercy? of redemptive revelation? of God's love for man? of Jesus' death on the cross? if all of these have God himself as their primal object and meaning? Within such a theology of reprobation and election, all of these concepts are emptied of the meaning they have in the gospel and given a foreign content.

Can the gospel of Hoeksema's theology be preached? Hardly. He has turned the gospel into a principle of divine power and causation which, without response to human, created conditions—and thus without reference to anything man says or does—actualizes the salvation of the elect and the damnation of the reprobate. Such a gospel can be announced—coolly, objectively, without pathos or human concern or tears—but it cannot be preached with persuasion, with the tears of Jesus and the anguish of Paul for his unbelieving fellow Jews.

When the Protestant Reformed Churches divided into two denominations in 1957, the issue that produced the split was a crisis of the pulpit. Separation occurred over the legitimacy of saying in the pulpit, "If you believe, God will save you." Hoeksema rejected this formulation because of its conditionality. He saw it as a concession to Arminianism and a surrender to conditionality of God's true sovereignty. Given his position, the crisis would have been theologically the same if the issue had been stated in reverse: "If you do not believe, God will damn you." Either expression was heretical because it endorsed the kind of conditionality Hoeksema rejected.

Hoeksema brought election and reprobation into the pulpit and in the process, theologically speaking, lost the gospel and came up with a form of gospel that the pulpit could not preach. This is not to say that the gospel is not heard in churches that follow his theology. The gospel is able to break through our theological mutations of it and gain a hearing for itself. Whatever our theological failures and distortions, the words of Jesus are still true: "He who hears you, hears me" (Luke 10:16).

Hoeksema was confronted with the criticism that the gospel, as he understood it in terms of election and reprobation, could not be preached to all men because it was really good news only for the elect. He responded by asserting that the gospel must indeed be preached to all men, but that its promise and proclamation of salvation are for the elect only. Consistent with this, he denied common grace (a kind of divine grace or favor for all men) and insisted that there is but one grace, saving grace, and that it is for the elect only. Why must the gospel be preached to all men then? Because it is the power that, through the means of preaching, actualizes the saving election of the elect and judgmentally actualizes the reprobation of the reprobate. How the gospel could, in terms of itself, without being conditioned by anything outside its own nature, be the effectuating cause of two such opposite results, Hoeksema did not explain. He left this problem of a dualistic, schizophrenic gospel for others to face. This is a serious piece of theological unfinished business on the agenda of Protestant Reformed theology. For the nature of the gospel is greatly obscured when it is defined as a power that *within its own internal terms* both saves and damns.

*   *   *

Cornelius Van Til of Westminster Theological Seminary was in general agreement with Hoeksema's theology. But Van Til saw Hoeksema's rejection of common grace, his rejection of the gospel as a well-meant offer of salvation, and his insistence that God always and only loves the elect and always and only hates the reprobate, as defects in Hoeksema's theology that resulted from a failure to take history seriously. If he had taken history seriously, urged Van Til, he would have recognized that man is on the move, in the process of becoming elect and reprobate individuals. Since this is so, God's attitude is also a moving, changing attitude, corresponding at a given moment to the point that a given man has reached in his historic development.

To these defects in Hoeksema's thought Van Til addressed his 1947 book *Common Grace*. In it he described man as on the move. Men begin as a human generality in the first man, Adam. All men existed in Adam, but only as a generality. At that earliest point in history, all men had everything in common. They had a common relationship to common grace, to the love of God, and to the gospel. Van Til did not indicate how this possession of all things in common related to election and reprobation. Yet this was the root of Hoeksema's alleged failure to take history seriously, for Hoeksema saw each man only in terms of his eternal election or reprobation and of God's eternal, unchanging attitude toward him.

Van Til contended that as history moves forward, mankind as a generality progressively turns into concrete elect and reprobate individuals. Moreover, within the life of each individual there is movement. The elect are progressively actualized as they self-consciously understand their reality as God's elect; the reprobate are progressively actualized as they self-consciously reject God. This process of individuation goes on until the end of history. At that point, all the elect and reprobate are actualized; and mankind as a generality ceases to exist. When mankind altogether ceases to exist as a generality, common grace as *common* and the gospel as a *general* offer of salvation also wholly cease to exist. At that point God has nothing but love for the elect and nothing but hatred for the reprobate. Prior to that, God's attitude—as expressed in common grace and in the gospel—is a mixture of both, with the ratio of love and hatred determined by the point reached by men in the historical process.

Thus there is a favorable divine attitude toward man in both common grace and in the gospel only at an *earlier* point in history. Earlier than what? Earlier than the achieved actuality of elect and reprobate men at any given moment in history. To the extent that both are not yet differentiated individuals, they are the objects of a common love and of a common offer of salvation. Or, to put it differently, the elect and reprobate have a common grace and common gospel to the degree that they are, at that moment in history, still mankind as a generality. This generality, however, cannot be saved, since it is progressively eliminated in history until it wholly disappears at the end. The church proclaiming the gospel must declare that God loves the elect more today than yesterday and the reprobate less. This is good news for the elect but bad news for the reprobate. But in biblical thought, the gospel is always good news and remains that whether or not men believe it. This elimination of mankind as a generality raises the question whether this concept ever indicated an actual human *reality*. The answer is clearly negative, for mankind as a generality does not last, nor can it be saved. It is a concept that merely indicates a "mode of existence," a mode without any actual existent.

Just how real are common grace and a general offer of salvation to all men, if these are real for all men only to the degree that they are not-yet real, individual men? Van Til's thought here cast a threatening shadow of unreality over mankind as a generality, over common grace, and over a universal offer of salvation.

This is a defect that haunts all decretal theology, as we shall see later. Recall again what happened to the concept of mercy in Hoeksema's thought. In order to maintain that God is unaffected by anything outside himself, he urged that God is merciful to himself, whereas the Bible thinks of mercy as something God shows to sinful man. To escape the idea that sin is an external situation to which God in his freedom chooses to respond, Hoeksema contends that God, in having mercy on man, is not responding in some way to a new situation because God has always had mercy for himself. But if mercy is understood as an internal attitude of God toward himself, the biblical reality of mercy is seriously threatened.

What energy triggers the process of differentiation by which mankind as a generality progressively becomes concrete, individual elect and reprobate men? For Hoeksema it is the preaching of the gospel. Preaching is a blessing for the elect, a means of damning the reprobate; the baptism of an elect infant is a blessing, for a reprobate infant a curse; rain and sunshine are in themselves good things, yet they are for the elect a blessing and for the reprobate a curse.

Unlike Hoeksema, Van Til endorses common grace and the general well-meant gospel offer of salvation. Yet, he defines both within the basic presuppositions of Hoeksema's theology, for he sees the dynamic that thrusts mankind out of generality into individual, actual elect and reprobate as common grace and the proclamation of the gospel's well-meant offer of salvation. The gospel, according to Van Til, is not only "the power of God for salvation to every one who has faith," it is also the power that produces the reprobate. A reprobate is not reprobate because he is a sinner and does not believe, but because of common grace and the well-meant offer of the gospel.

So how *real* are common grace and the well-meant gospel offer of salvation on Van Til's view? If the proclamation of the gospel's well-meant offer of salvation does in fact, and according to the gospel's inherent nature, effect the differentiation of mankind as a generality into reprobate as well as elect, if common grace "comes upon the non-believer that he might crucify to himself the Son of God afresh,"[5] do these two concepts have any reality, any definable content?

When Van Til and Hoeksema speak this way, they contend that they are articulating authentic Reformed theology. Their differences come within the context of a much deeper agreement. Both expound a decretal theology in which God's decree is not identified with his freedom, but with his essence, and thus with God himself. On this position God himself is—and is in the same manner *(in eodem modo)*—the

---

5 *Common Grace*, p. 95.

cause and therefore the explanation and rationale of "whatsoever comes to pass," including election and reprobation—a
principle the Canons of Dort reject. It is evident that nothing
in decretal theology is new, special, unique, specifically gracious, truly gospel, that everything is essentially neutral, of
the same nature and accomplished "in the same manner."
For Van Til common grace and the gospel *produce* both elect
and reprobate men; in Hoeksema, preaching and infant baptism both bless the elect and curse the reprobate.

Hoeksema grappled with the question of how the gospel
could be preached to all men if it is good news only for the
elect. Given his understanding of the decree of God, the best
he could do was assert that the gospel was for the elect only.
This left him with the problem of how to preach the gospel
to all men, if its promise is only for some. He solved this
problem by reducing preaching to mere announcement. Such
a view is a far cry from the biblical portrait of preaching as a
peculiar speech of the church that is dynamic, creative,
judgmental, a voice of the church, in which, according to
Jesus, "he who hears you, hears me."

Van Til recognized that a proclamation of the gospel to all
men which is merely an announcement of the gospel was
highly unsatisfactory because it was a theological verbalism
that obscured rather than solved the problem. So he offered
his understanding of the gospel to show that it could indeed
be preached and not merely announced to all men. But he
was no more successful than Hoeksema. No less than Hoeksema, he viewed the gospel in terms of an eternal election and
reprobation that must be interpreted in terms of an all-comprehensive decree that lies behind it. Despite Van Til's appeal
to history and his criticism of Hoeksema for failing to take it
seriously, despite his more sophisticated theological and philosophical treatment of the problem, Van Til came out theologically at precisely the same point where Hoeksema had
come out by a simpler and more direct route. For Van Til no
less than for Hoeksema, the nature of the gospel and the
purpose of its proclamation was to put the elect in heaven
and the reprobates in hell. Van Til's appeal to history did
nothing more than urge that God takes time and employs

process to achieve election and reprobation through the preaching of the gospel.

Hoeksema and Van Til have made the most comprehensive and sophisticated attempts to bridge the gap between election and preaching. None tried harder, none wrestled more seriously and vigorously with this problem. Compared to their efforts, those of the seventeenth-century Scottish and the eighteenth-century Dutch Reformed theologians were simplistic and naive. Yet for all their effort, Hoeksema and Van Til were no more successful than their Scottish and Dutch predecessors. Once one commits himself to the decree of decretal theology, it is theologically impossible for him to allow, justify, or explain preaching the gospel to all men. So, too, it is impossible for him to bring election into the pulpit.

CHAPTER III

The Source of the Gap

We saw in the preceeding chapter that in pulpits committed to Arminian theology election has the place of an appendage. Gaining entree after the sermon, election is not really preached. This criticism, however, is not likely to disturb the informed Arminian, for he knows that the sound of election is scarcely heard in Reformed pulpits either. Let us now turn to the question why this is so.

An examination of the difficulties, cited in the preceding chapter, that Reformed thought had with election and preaching reveals that they all stem from the idea of non-election. If election, like the gospel, could be preached to all men, these difficulties would not have arisen. But if election is for the elect only, whereas the gospel is to be proclaimed to all men, what keeps election and preaching apart is non-election, or reprobation. Reformed theologians never solved the problem of "an election for some and a gospel for all." Their sophisticated and ingenious attempts to resolve the difficulties and produce a preachable theology of election lie largely forgotten in the past, of historical interest only. But the theological problem itself remains. At the practical level, in the pulpit, the problem is resolved by simply ignoring election—a dangerous disposition of the problem, for election belongs to the core of the gospel. And persistent silence about election will open the Reformed pulpit to Arminianism.

Simply stated, reprobation gets in the way of every attempt to take election seriously because in traditional Reformed theology *reprobation is always there*. According to this tradition, election and reprobation are interrelated and inseparable concepts. To believe in election is also to believe in reprobation. To reject one is to reject both. Any intermediate position, any variant of a simple Yes to both, is instinctively designated as a surrender to Arminian theology. Whether this kinship between election and reprobation represents the inner motif of Reformed theology rather than a vagrant development of it is a much debated subject, and a question that calls for careful examination and evaluation.

Those who argue that election necessarily involves reprobation see their position as very simple, logical, even axiomatic. But the history of Reformed thought shows that consensus ends with this initial step, for there is little agreement among Reformed theologians as to precisely *how* election and reprobation are interrelated. For once the simple datum of election joined with reprobation is accepted, nothing else is simple.

The Conclusion of the Canons of Dort explicitly rejects—in fact, *detests*—the position that election and reprobation are related "in the same manner" (*in eodem modo*). God does not elect men in the same manner in which he rejects men. Election and reprobation are not simply two sides of the same coin. By rejecting the "in the same manner," the Canons destroy the argument that the endorsement of a proper doctrine of election is automatically also an endorsement of a proper doctrine of reprobation. The relationship of election and reprobation is not a simple one, like two sides of the same coin, or the simple affirmation that one logically implies the other.[1]

If the Canons, by rejecting the "in the same manner," give

---

[1] In discussing the counsel of God Bavinck repeatedly repudiates the notion that God elects and reprobates in the same manner. Reprobation is not the same kind of divine act as election, nor is reprobation demanded by the fact that all things must glorify God. Neither the fact or nature of reprobation derives logically from the fact and nature of election. *Gereformeerde Dogmatiek*, I, 405f. Berkhof goes far beyond this in offering "proof" of reprobation: "The doctrine of reprobation naturally follows from the logic of the situation. The decree of election inevitably implies the decree of reprobation." *Systematic Theology*, p. 117.

election a privileged footing, the general tendency of seven-
teenth- and eighteenth-century scholastic Reformed theology
was to give election and reprobation equal footing. The
Canons' imbalance between election and reprobation was thus
often lost; the logic of reprobation, as we shall see later,
triumphed over election. When this happened, a demonic
element was introduced into some Reformed theologies, as is
inevitable when the relation between election and reprobation is taken to be one of mutuality, for such mutuality tears
the gospel apart.

An example of this emergence of the demonic can be seen
in Hoeksema's theology. According to Hoeksema, God decreed to reveal in Christ his own covenantal life. Everything
else in God's all-comprehensive decree is a means to that end.
Since Christ and the community of the elect reflect God's
inner covenantal life, election at this point in his thought has
a priority. Within the pattern of the decree, reprobation also
serves the purpose of election, "as the chaff serves the ripen-
ing of the wheat."[2] Here again election has the priority. But
Hoeksema further holds that God had to reject some if he
was to elect some. Reprobation was absolutely necessary for
the election. "Rejection exists to realize election: rejection
was necessary to bring the elect to the glory which God had
ordained for them in His infinite love."[3]

Now if God must damn some in order to elect and bless
others, he is not sovereignly free in his grace. But this means
that reprobation has really triumphed over election, for reprobation and human damnation are required for a disclosure
of the nature of God's covenantal life. God was obliged to
reprobate. He could not do otherwise. How forthrightly, and
with what confidence, decretal theologians delimit the possibilities of the sovereign God! G. C. Berkouwer finds this
"frightening and alarming."[4] It is a clear instance of how
scholastic decretal theologians must read alien elements into
God.

A different construction of the relation between election

2 *Reformed Dogmatics*, p. 165.
3 *De Plaats der Verwerping in de Verkondiging des Evangelies* (1917), p. 16.
4 *Divine Election*, p. 207n.

and reprobation is found in the theology of Karl Barth. Barth held that all men are both reprobated and elected in Jesus Christ, who is also both reprobate and elect. But in this instance election is given privileged footing, for election in Barth overcomes reprobation. Election bespeaks a triumph of grace, and so Barth's theology came to be designated by his critics as a "triumphant theology." Emil Brunner disagreed with Barth and with Reformed theology generally. He held to eternal election but denied that the Bible teaches eternal reprobation.[5] Thus Brunner solved the problem of relationship by denying that there is a decree of reprobation to which election is inherently related.

These examples illustrate that there has been wide disagreement about the relationship of election to reprobation both among conservative and among less conservative Reformed theologians. Such variety dispels the naive popular notion that the truth about election and reprobation is quite simple and has always been uniformly held and defined in the Reformed theological tradition.

* * *

Nonetheless, there is a strand in the Reformed theological tradition, particularly visible in the decretal theology that developed after Calvin, in which election and reprobation are so compounded that reprobation becomes an ingredient of election. The congenital inseparability of the two comes to expression in the use given to the term predestination. Scripture speaks explicitly of a predestination to life but not to death. However, this did not make Reformed theologians hesitant about using the term to denote a predestination to death, or indeed about using it to cover "whatsoever comes to pass." By expanding the term, these theologians blurred the distinction between election and whatever comes to pass, dissociated "predestination" from "life," and buried the Canons' rejection of the "in the same manner" far from thought and memory. (Louis Berkhof's *Systematic Theology* does not mention the "in the same manner," though it is clearly

5 *Dogmatics*, I (*The Christian Doctrine of God*), 331-339.

indispensable to an understanding of the Canons.) God was increasingly seen as determining alike the destiny of the amoral sparrow, the unbelief of the reprobate, and the faith of the elect. And the all-embracing term predestination blurred the distinction between election and reprobation.

The inclusion of election and reprobation as mere instances of a cosmic, wall-to-wall doctrine of predestination, eased the transfer of election and reprobation back into the first locus of systematic theology, in which the doctrine of God is discussed. Calvin had rescued election and reprobation from there, where scholastic orthodoxy had treated it, and had transferred it to the locus of soteriology, where election and reprobation are discussed in the context of man's sin and God's grace. In this soteriological context, where election and reprobation are defined within those matters that constitute the salvation wrought by God in Christ, election and reprobation cannot be reduced to the indistinguishable components of the all-embracing decree of scholastic decretal theology.

But Calvin's advance beyond medieval scholasticism was soon squandered. His valuable biblical perspective was negated when Beza his successor, falling back into medieval scholasticism, returned election and reprobation to a place within a general concept of predestination, assigned predestination to the locus of the doctrine of God, and proceeded to develop a decretal theology that he bequeathed to a seventeenth- and eighteenth-century Reformed scholasticism that uncritically accepted him over Calvin. Since then the doctrine of election has been treated by most systematic theologians not in soteriology but in systematic theology's first locus.

This in turn encouraged defining election and reprobation merely in terms of divine sovereignty. Both were increasingly defined as hardly-to-be-distinguished aspects of a divine sovereignty that predestines every datum of created reality. More and more, election was defined apart from grace, and the *sovereign grace* with which the Reformation was concerned came increasingly to be displaced by mere sovereignty. Reprobation for its part was increasingly defined apart from sin, again, in terms of straight sovereignty.

The tendency to make divine sovereignty alone definitive of election and reprobation made it easy for Reformed scholasticism to adopt the distinctive feature of the prevailing Newtonian natural science, which saw the world as a mechanical universe where every movement occurs through the principle of causality and God is sovereign over all things because he is the cause of all things. To be sure Reformed scholastics hesitated when they thought about sin, but not enough. They declined to call God the "author" of sin; some held that he willed it "in a sense," and others hesitated only long enough to make that assertion before going on to affirm that God is nonetheless the final and ultimate cause of sin. Although God was said to be the ultimate cause of sin, the guilt of sin was said to be all and only man's. Thus these theologians projected causality without responsibility. God could cause sin, but could not be responsible for it. Although man was regarded as only a secondary cause of sin, his guilt was not secondary, nor primary, but total and exclusive.

Here was a reduction of election, seen as inseparable from reprobation, to a generalized predestination defined in terms of a mere divine sovereignty made effective through divine causality. This distorted profoundly the doctrines of election and reprobation. The former is, in fact, simply unknowable apart from God's grace; and the latter is equally unknowable apart from the realities of human sin and guilt and divine justice as a reaction to them. Yet it was precisely because of this theological reductionism that Reformed theologians often found it possible to form a single definition of election and reprobation. Such single definitions of election and reprobation can be found in theological writings, and indeed, they are inherent in the initial statement of the supralapsarian's outline of the logical stages of God's decree. But it should be recognized that such single definitions—as well as the reductionism that makes them possible—are built on accepting the "in the same manner," which the Canons explicitly reject.

If one considers the nature of election and the quite different nature of reprobation, one would not expect that any single definition would be able to cover the two realities. Nor would one expect that the positive act of election could logically and automatically be regarded as positing reprobation. Yet logic here played a powerful role, and since the days of Reformed scholasticism, election and reprobation have been increasingly regarded as logical implicates, and thus as two concepts that mesh in rational harmony.

Justification for a single definition that served both equally well was sought in the Canons of Dort. The Canons do, as a matter of fact, discuss election and reprobation together, for example, in Head I, and they do so by projecting a single decree that includes both. "That some receive the gift of faith and others do not receive it, proceeds from God's eternal decree" (Art. 6). Later in the same article, after asserting that God "softens the hearts of the elect" and "leaves the non-elect in his just judgment to their own wickedness and obduracy," the Canons describe this dual action as God's "righteous discrimination between men," and declare this to be "that decree of election and reprobation revealed in the Word of God."

The Canons do indeed speak of a single decree. First of all, they do so because they do not accept the multiple decrees of the Arminian theology that they take great pains to reject. Second, the Bible itself knows of no plurality of divine decrees. Moreover, the Canons provide no supportive evidence for the insistence by some latter-day Reformed theologians that election and reprobation logically imply each other, that "reprobation naturally follows from the logic of the situation [and] the decree of election inevitably implies the decree of reprobation" (Berkhof); or that election presupposes reprobation (Hoeksema); or that election and reprobation are beyond all doubt the teaching not only of the Bible, but also "of reason" (Lorraine Boettner).[6] The Canons' insistence that God does not elect and reprobate "in the

---

[6] *The Reformed Doctrine of Predestination* (11th ed.), p. 95. Boettner's book (first published in 1932) has been widely used in conservative Reformed theological circles. Its view of election is one of the most rationalistic extant. Boettner's announced purpose is "to show that . . . [the Reformed faith] is beyond all doubt the teaching of the Bible and of reason" (p. 1). His method is to operate from certain basic principles, chief of which is the Westminster Confession's teaching that God absolutely and unconditionally determines, not merely man's salvation but "whatsoever comes to pass." Boettner's view of election is so completely under the governance of the principle of an all-embracing predestination that his concept of election becomes so expansive as to be virtually meaningless.

same manner" rules out the legitimacy of election and reprobation in terms of logical relationships.

If what the Canons (particularly I, 6) say about the granting of faith to some men and not to others is interpreted in terms of the single decree of a *later* decretal theology, they appear to teach that God is the cause of some men's unbelief. But this is a profound distortion of the single decree as found there. The Canons explicitly reject the idea that God is in any sense the cause of sin and unbelief. According to the Synod of Dort, it is not the case that God elects and reprobates "in the same manner"; thus the rationale that God's decree equally accounts for and explains why some men believe and some do not is excluded. The teaching of the Canons that God elects in one way and reprobates in another breaks every form of logical symmetry or parallelism between election and reprobation.

It is true that the Canons' use of a "single decree" provided the *verbal* possibility for latter-day decretal theologians to appeal to the Canons for support of their scholastic, rationalistic understanding of election and reprobation. But the Canons can hardly be faulted because some theologians read them in terms of a post-Dort scholasticism that accepted the "*in eodem modo*," which the Canons rejected.

The theology of Berkhof, Hoeksema, Van Til, and Boettner has been decisively shaped by a disregard of the "not in the same manner." For the most part, their writings do not even mention it, although the rejection of the "not in the same manner" is part of the Conclusions of the Canons. This disregard has made it possible to propagate with considerable popular success the idea that the Canons can easily be interpreted in supralapsarian terms.

*   *   *

Reformed scholasticism arose hard on the heels of the Reformation. This can be seen in the theology of Beza, Calvin's successor at Geneva, and in the Westminster Confession (1647), which, coming nearly three decades later than the Canons of Dort, was closer to the heyday of Reformed scholasticism. Like the Canons, the Westminster Confession dealt with election and reprobation, but, unlike the Canons, it did so only after it had first posited a single decree (De Aeterno Dei Decreto, Chapter III) although the American edition of this Confession speaks, in the plural, of decrees. This single decree of the Westminster Confession, unlike that of the Canons, which refers only to election and reprobation, refers to "whatsoever comes to pass."

This Westminster approach to election and reprobation—first constructing a doctrine of the predestination of all things and then dealing with election and reprobation within the terms of this general predestination—both reflected an earlier scholasticism and encouraged Reformed scholasticism to do the same. It had unhappy consequences. It encouraged the placement of the doctrine of election and reprobation in the doctrine of God. This in turn encouraged the search for a first cause and thus for an explanation of sin and of reprobation in God. Interpreting election and reprobation within the terms of a general predestination also tended to confuse matters by making predestination, election, and reprobation synonymous terms. It led Abraham Kuyper to speak of the election of birds and flowers,[7] and Lorraine Boettner to speak of the election of America.[8] It also helped create the notion that the Bible uses the language of predestination to death as well as predestination to life. The fact—which comes as a surprise to many—that the Bible uses a verb meaning "to elect" but none meaning "to reprobate" tended to be obscured.

This tendency to blend election and reprobation and to subsume both under a single decree that determines all things made it difficult for the Reformed pulpit to preach sermons on election. In turn, the idea that election is simply one instance of a general predestination that determines birds and flowers and the price of rhubarb on tomorrow's market made the pulpit's silence about election seem less serious than it is.

The word "predestination" refers to something's destiny being determined before it is reached. Divine predestination

---

7 *The Stone Lectures on Calvinism*, p. 272.
8 *Op. cit.*, p. 88.

means, then, that God determines the destiny of whatever is predestined before that destiny is reached. So the *pre* in predestination includes whatever is prior to the destiny; it therefore includes God's priority over all created and historical reality—which is an expression of God's freedom—and no less over whatever in the created and fallen world God in his freedom wills to bring to a particular destiny.

Since predestination refers to the final destiny of whatever is predestined, it cannot be defined in terms of "whatsoever comes to pass." One of the things that has come to pass is the act of God by which the world was created. But the *creation* of the world is not the *predestination* of the world. God's creative act constitutes the origin of the world, and the origin of the world is not the destiny of the world. To identify the two is to deny the history of the world; indeed, it is to deny that anything other than the creation of the world has come to pass. Nor is the fall of the world into sin to be described as the world's predetermined *destiny;* this would be to deny that Christ died to save and bring the world to its final destiny in spite of the fall.

When predestination is defined as God's eternal determination of "whatsoever comes to pass," the dimension of the historical, which is of the very fabric of Christianity, is lost. Predestination defined in terms, not of what God in his freedom achieved by and through what comes to pass, but in terms of *whatever* comes to pass, cannot carry the meaning of biblical history and eschatology.

Paul provides the classic biblical definition of predestination in the latter part of Romans 8. Two features of Paul's definition are especially noteworthy. First, he defines predestination without any mention of God's creation of the world or man's fall into sin. Thus the classic biblical definition of predestination is without reference to "whatever comes to pass."

Second, instead of defining God's predestination in terms of "whatsoever comes to pass," Paul urges that God can and does make all things work for the good of those who love God, that nothing that comes to pass—whether tribulation, anguish, persecution, famine, nakedness, peril, sword, death, life, angels, principalities, things present, things to come, powers, height, depth, or any other creature—can separate us from God's love or thwart God's predestined purpose. Why not? Because in all these things we are more than *conquerors* through Christ.

Predestination is not definable in terms of "whatsoever comes to pass." On the contrary, Paul defines predestination *without reference to* some things that have come to pass—namely, creation and the fall—and *in reference to* Christ's conquering much that has come to pass that is contrary to what God has predestined for all those who love him.

Decretal theologians cannot take seriously the term "come to pass." For if every event is itself destiny, then nothing moves toward a destiny, and nothing comes to pass in the historical sense. If everything in history is destiny (destination), then there is no historical datum that *moves* towards its destiny. If the future is now, then there is no predestination, and every man and institution may face the future either with proud defiance or despairing hopelessness, whichever his present status allows.

In an authentic view of predestination there is an inherent reference to the future. The term is essentially an historical one. As such it is open to preaching, for preaching also is oriented toward the future.

CHAPTER IV

The Single Decree

Reformed theologians have long held to a single divine decree of election, as opposed to a multiple decree. Francis Turretin argued for the single decree in his *Institutio Theologiae Elencticae;* Leonardus Riissenius did so in his *Summa Theologiae;* the Westminster Confession, as we noted in the last chapter, does so; and the Canons of Dort urge the singularity of God's decree against Arminian theologians who held to multiple decrees.

According to the Canons, Arminianism holds to "various kinds of election of God unto eternal life: the one general and indefinite, the other particular and definite. . . . " The "general and indefinite" election of God, which elects all men in general but no man in particular, is as abstract and void of all meaning as some Reformed constructions, such as that which contends that the gospel is by nature for the elect only but that it is also preachable to all men; or that which sees the gospel as good news for "mankind as a generality," though this generality is not savable since the nature of the gospel is to eliminate the generality by turning it into actual individuals differentiated as elect and reprobate; or, to mention one more, the 1924 contention of the Christian Reformed Church that the preaching of the gospel to all men as a well-meant offer of salvation proves the reality of a common, non-saving grace of God for all men. These abstract and essentially meaningless formulas, intended to relate the Reformed doctrine of reprobation with a gospel that must be

preached to all, are as abstract and meaningless as the Arminian attempts to define election within a recognition that not
all men are saved.

The second kind of election—the "particular and definite"—was defined by Arminian theology, to use the words
of the Canons, as "either incomplete, revocable, non-decisive,
and conditional, or complete, irrevocable, decisive, and absolute" (I, Rej. 2), which is to say that Arminian theology gives
two exactly opposite definitions to the same divine elective
act. They did so to comply with their belief that some men
truly believe but only for a time—in other words, not all
saints persevere in the faith. But this notion of election is at
least as unacceptable and as meaningless as the attempt by
Reformed thought to define election and reprobation by a
single definition. Like Reformed theology, Arminianism tried
to formulate a single definition of election to reflect their
common admission that not all men are saved. And both
produced—each in its own way—a mere verbal formula.

Arminianism also held that there is one decree to election
and another decree to faith, reflecting the Arminian tenet
that God's election is a response to man's decision to believe.
The Canons rightly reject this, asserting that "there are not
various decrees of election but one." And they hold this as
true "since the Scripture declares the good pleasure, purpose,
and counsel of the divine will to be one" (I, 8).

Whether it is possible to hold to a single decree that
includes both election and reprobation and to hold at the
same time that God does not elect and reprobate "in the
same manner" is a rhetorical question. If God elects in one
manner and rejects in another, then it is impossible to attach
any actual meaning to the singularity of the divine decree. It
seems clear that the rejection of the "in the same manner"
introduces a distinction into the concept of singularity that
makes the quality of singularity highly problematic. So while
the insistence on a single as opposed to a multiple decree was
useful in debate with the Arminians, it also undermines the
Canons' rejection of the "in the same manner."

In its insistence on a single decree—quite apart from
whether election and reprobation constitute a single decree—
the Canons have support in the language of Scripture. Scrip-

ture always speaks of God's decree (purpose, counsel, good
pleasure, will) in the singular, never in the plural. Paul speaks
of the "counsel of [God's] will" (Eph. 1:11), of the "purpose of his will" (Eph. 1:5), of "the mystery of God, even
Christ" (Col. 2:2), and of "the eternal purpose which [God]
has realized in Christ" (Eph. 3:11). The psalmist defines the
decree of the Lord with the words, "You are my Son, today I
have begotten you. Ask of me, and I will make the nations
your heritage, and the ends of the earth your possession" (Ps.
2:7-8). The language is always singular, never plural. The
Bible, accordingly, uses the language "predestination to life"
but does not speak of predestination to death. God does not
reveal two eternal purposes in Christ, nor two—not to say
more—good pleasures or counsels of his will, either in or
outside of Christ. The psalmist says, "Thou dost guide me
with thy counsel" (Ps. 73:24), and Isaiah designates Christ as
"Wonderful Counselor" (9:6). Christ would be a poor counselor and the psalmist would have poor guidance if God's
counsel and decree were dualistically structured. A dualistic
divine decree, oriented to more than one goal, would be
schizophrenic and antithetically structured. It would indicate that God does not know what he wants or what he is
pursuing. Such a decree would hardly be much of a guide
for poor sinners seeking direction and needing knowledge
of God's purpose for their lives.

Reformed theologians also insisted on the single character
of God's decree against Lutheran theology, which generally
followed Luther in making a distinction between God's
proper work and his *strange* work (see Isa. 28:21). Love and
grace exemplify God's proper work; judgment and holiness
his strange work. Lutheranism sees a tension between these
proper and strange works—between law and gospel, grace and
justice, love and holiness. According to Helmut Thielicke,
Lutheran theology acknowledges that these contradictions
reside in God himself. "Indeed, the gospel itself can be traced
to this fundamental contradiction within God himself."[1]

Reformed theology did not regard law and gospel as
contradictory terms, Thielicke says, and was unwilling to

[1] *Theological Ethics: Politics*, A Library of Protestant Thought, III, 575.

regard such a dualism and contradiction as grounded in God himself. Reformed theology maintained the single character of the divine decree against Lutheranism for reasons different from those to which it appealed in its arguments against Arminian theology. While Lutheranism has held to this dualistic, contradictory character of God's decree out of awareness of the reality of contradictions in history—a reality that slips through the fingers of the Reformed grasp of the single divine decree—it did so at the cost of reading the contradictions of history into the decree of God and into God himself. By doing so it made God's decree cover "whatsoever comes to pass." So the logic of the Lutheran position is: history confronts us with contradictions; God's decree must include these contradictions, for it must have (as Reformed theology also insisted) full coverage of all that occurs. Since God's decree reflects what God is in himself (also following the scholastic tradition of Reformed theology) the contradictions of history must obtain within God himself. So it is that Thielicke can say that the law-grace contradictions of the gospel "can be traced to this fundamental contradiction within God himself." As Lutheranism sees it, God's strange work is grounded in his very nature no less than his proper work. Thus both Reformed and Lutheran theology arrive at very opposite positions out of the same motif.

Lutheran theology, recognizing the contradictions of history lying between God's "proper" and "strange" work, relates both to the divine decree and thereby to God himself. Reformed theology, in the name of a single decree, denies God's "strange" work in history, regarding it instead as his proper work, and thus ends up interjecting the same contradictions into God as does Lutheranism. But Lutheranism admits it, and Reformed theology denies it. Both are in fact caught in the same trap. Both miss the distinctive feature of God's decree—its essential historicity, which derives from, is determined by, and expresses God's freedom, not in the abstract, but in its concrete and free exercise. Lutheranism took history seriously at the cost of God; Reformed thought took God and his eternality seriously at the cost of history.

Both Lutheranism and Reformed theology failed because they did not recognize that the eternal decree of the eternal

God was the *single* decree of God to *go historical,* a free
exercise of God's freedom to move out of himself creatively
toward and into both creation and redemption. This unique,
wondrous, most gracious character of God's decree is not
expressed in the attempt by Lutheranism to read the contradictions of history back into God, nor in the Reformed
attempt to dissolve the contradictions by denying that they
are contradictory because they are willed by God. The solution to this problem of both Lutheran and Reformed thought
lies in a recognition that the decree of God has its secret
neither in the eternality of God nor in the fact of history, but
in that exercise of divine freedom by which God, through
creation and incarnation, moved out of himself to become
historical. God as such does not explain history, as Reformed
theology has long thought. Nor is history a direct commentary on the nature of God, as Lutheran theology has long
thought. The truth lies between the two views and differs
profoundly from both. The truth lies in that freedom of God
by which he decided to go historical.

This is a most important discussion for our purposes,
because the basic position of this writing lies in a specific
view of God's freedom, according to which the divine decree
is both eternal and historical. The time-eternity problem has
always been difficult for Christian theology. Decretal theologies in particular have wrestled to obtain at least some
understanding of how God's eternal decree relates to the
realities of history. Before we investigate this complex subject more fully, we must make a closer examination of the
meaning of the single decree in the Reformed tradition,
particularly as it appeared in Francis Turretin.[2]

*   *   *

The single decree in the Reformed tradition meant a
rejection of the multiple, conditional decree of Arminian
theology and of the Lutheran idea that the dualistic tensions

---

[2] *Institutio Theologiae Elencticae,* Locus IV, Question I, X, xvii. Cf. *Reformed
Dogmatics,* edited by John W. Beardslee III, which contains what Beardslee
believes "is the only publication of any part of his [Turretin's] work in English
before now."

and contradictions between law and gospel, love and holiness, God's strange and proper work, are located in God himself. The single decree means much more than this, and much more than the simple affirmation that God's decree has a single purpose or goal. In Reformed thought the singularity of God's decree is more a matter of the nature of the decree than its goal.

We may begin by pointing out that the nature of the singularity of God's decree in Reformed thought is such that for our finite minds it is unthinkable. Though we can and do use the term, we cannot, so to speak, wrap our minds around this concept. Whenever we reflect on the single decree, we break the decree up into pieces and think decrees—a decree to create, a decree to redeem, a decree to elect, a decree to reprobate. So we cannot reflect on the single decree nor convey our reflections without making distinctions that do not in fact characterize the decree. This inability was explained by man's finitude: "Our finite comprehension," says Berkhof, "constrains us to make distinctions and this accounts for the fact that we often speak of the decrees of God in the plural. . . . This manner of speaking is perfectly legitimate, provided we do not lose sight of the unity of the divine decree, and of the inseparable connection of the various decrees."[3]

Berkhof bows here not to revelation but to the finitude of the human mind. He fails, however, to confront what is really at stake: the possibility of *any* human knowledge of God's decree. If God's single decree has no distinguishable parts, then we can have no knowledge of the single decree. We can neither think about it or talk about it. Again, if the single decree has no content for us that we can reflectively think and speak about unless we break it up into distinguishable parts, the single decree, as it is in itself, has for our minds neither reality nor content. The most we can do is utter the words "single decree." If our reflection breaks the singularity of the decree into parts, we are no longer reflecting on the *single* decree, for it, by definition, has no parts. And when Berkhof justifies our breaking up the

[3] *Systematic Theology*, p. 102.

single decree as "perfectly legitimate, provided we do not
lose sight of the unity of the divine decree," he is asking us to
keep in sight what we never saw, to remember what we never
had knowledge of.

We shall discover more and more in this chapter how large
a role the single decree has played in much of traditional
Reformed theology. One of the early Reformed theologians
to urge the single character of God's decree was Francis
Turretin (1623-87), a Reformed professor of theology at
Geneva. Turretin said it this way: "The decrees of God are
not intrinsically many as differences in God, although they
are different extrinsically [that is, to us]; so that what is
formally different in finite beings is by way of eminence
identified in the infinite being."[3a] In other words, Turretin
contends that God's decree as it exists in God is singular, but
can only appear to our minds as plural. The difference, he
says, is only *formal.*

This assertion is word-play. For if God's decree is in its
nature singular but appears to finite minds as plural, the
difference between the decree and our knowledge of it is not
merely formal, but material and substantive. If it were not a
substantive difference, the singularity of the decree would
mean nothing. The difference between what the single decree
is and our knowledge of what it is, is so great that the
singularity of the decree falls outside the possibilities of
human knowledge.

Thus, traditional Reformed decretal thought confronts us
with a perplexing phenomenon. It takes the singularity of
God's decree to be basic and determinative of theology, a
touchstone of orthodoxy, yet it frankly acknowledges that
this distinctive inherent feature of the decree is something we
cannot even think.

Before we proceed to see just how large a role this decree
has played in Reformed theology, let us consider one further
implication of Turretin's statement. What he says suggests the
impossibility of any divine movement or action to become
man. If a single decree as intrinsic—that is, as it is in God—
cannot become extrinsic—that is, present outside of God in

[3a] Locus IV, Question I, xvii.

the context of the finite and created—without ceasing to be
what it is in God, namely, simple, then the Incarnation also
appears to be impossible. Admittedly, the Incarnation confronts us with more than we can fully understand. Yet the
Council of Nicea insisted that in the Incarnation God became
man without ceasing to be God. It affirmed that God could
be extrinsically what he is intrinsically. In effect Turretin
denies this when he insists that the intrinsic, simple character
of God's decree is lost when it becomes extrinsic and present
in history and in our thought. If we were to understand the
Incarnation in the way Turretin defines the transition of the
single decree from intrinsic to extrinsic, we would lose the
Incarnation just as truly as we lose all knowledge of the
singularity of God's decree.

In spite of the specter of unknowability, Reformed theology holds to the singularity of God's decree out of the
conviction that a *divine* decree must bear the character of the
divine. Since God is a simple being, not a composite of
multiple parts, the divine decree must also be a simple, single
act. The decretive act, therefore, is not composed of individual resolves, separable items, distinguishable moments. The
decree is a simple, single act in the same sense in which God
is a simple, singular being. When filtered through human
reflection, the single decree is fractured into diverse distinguishable items and moments. But this multiplicity of discrete distinguishable items and moments is only real for our
finite minds. In itself the decree is the very opposite. It is as
simple and without parts as God himself is simple and without parts. Since the decree is God's act, it must bear, Reformed orthodoxy maintained, the feature of deity.

The way Reformed theology deals with the attributes of
God is illustrative. Reformed theologians are not altogether
comfortable with the term "attributes." For one thing, it
carries the suggestion that the divine attributes are something
added to the nature of God. But furthermore it suggests that
the being of God is not simple but is marked by the various
distinctions suggested by the individual attributes. Hence any
comprehensive Reformed discussion about the attributes of
God usually includes the caveat that the fulness of God is in
each attribute and that each attribute is the fulness of God.

This is a warning that God's simplicity must not be threatened by the idea of multiplicity that is suggested by the term "attributes." God's only "attribute" is his singularity or simplicity. To speak of attributes is only a condescension to the finitude of man and his power of reflection. Similarly, God's decree is said to be a simple, singular decree.

In fact, Reformed theology has been much freer in its use of the divine attributes than it has with the distinctions that the finitude of our minds attributes to the decree of God. Reformed theology has not constructed a theology of the simplicity of God, but it has constructed a theology based on the singularity of the divine decree. Had it attempted to do the former, it would have produced a doctrine of God as empty and abstract as its theology of a single decree turned out to be.

If the single decree is such that the distinctions finite minds inevitably make in all thought and reflection on it do not in fact characterize it, a number of things follow.

First, election and reprobation, although they appear distinguishable to our finite minds, are in reality also indistinguishable. They are then one and the same thing in God's decree and for God himself. If this is true, both can properly be subsumed under a general concept of predestination and both can be defined by a single definition without reference to man's sin or God's grace and justice. And then all the debate about election and reprobation, infra- and supralapsarianism, conditional and unconditional theology should cease, because it is much ado about nothing. As a matter of historical fact, this is just about what has happened to the great controversies within the Reformed churches. Once the theological turbulence was over, the Reformed churches carried on much as if it had never occurred. Who in the Reformed churches today pays serious attention to those typically Reformed controversies about election and reprobation, the gospel as an offer, common grace, and other related controversies of the past?

Second, if the single decree has no distinguishable elements, yet determines all things and whatever comes to pass, the distinctions that mark all created reality and all the moments of history are ultimately unreal no matter how they appear to our finitude. In that case, either all created reality and history is one single, undefinable, indistinguishable datum that exists "in the same manner" without differentiation, or the distinctions that characterize all created reality in space and time fall outside of a single decree that allegedly determines all things. Either reality is without distinctions because it is determined by a decree that has no distinctions, or the distinctions that differentiate reality in space and time fall outside this single decree. The Reformed formulation of the single decree is susceptible to this devastating internal criticism. Its doctrine of the single decree is internally inconsistent and self-contradictory. Thus Reformed decretal theology is required either to follow the tradition of philosophical idealism and deny reality in the interest of an ideational divine decree, or to fall into the lap of Arminianism and allow such distinctions as that of election and reprobation to reside in something outside the decree of God.

Third, if the single decree is without distinguishable differentiation of fact or movement, it cannot be distinguished from God. It is divine and eternal, timeless and immutable. Then "God is all," to use a phrase commonly used by scholastic theology in its discussions about God's decree, either in the pantheistic sense that God is everything, or in the essentially skeptical sense of rationalistic idealism that nothing is real except God. Either possible alternative is a profoundly unbiblical view of God's decree.

The scholastic contention that God's decree, because it was *divine,* is as simple and singular as God himself was bolstered in Reformed thought by an appeal to the nature of God's knowledge. The motivation behind this contention was to undo the position of the Arminians, who held that God does not *determine* but simply *foreknows* what will occur in the future, and on the basis of this foreknowledge makes separate, successive decrees as responsive adjustments to what man does or fails to do. Thus, for example, the Arminians held that God decreed to elect all men and then, in response to the unbelief of many men, decreed to elect only those who believe. Reformed thought found this unacceptable, for it surrenders the truth of man's salvation by grace alone. But if the religious instinct of the Reformed theologians was right, they nonetheless forged their argument about the nature of God's knowledge in such a way as to constitute another step toward identifying God's decree with God himself.

God's knowledge, Reformed theologians urged, is unlike our knowledge. In our knowing we think step by step, moving from one idea to another, from cause to effect, from premise to conclusion. In short, our thinking involves time; it moves through successive moments. God, however, knows all things eternally and instantaneously, immediately and simultaneously. In his knowledge there are no parts, no succession, no movement from subject to predicate, no progression from one idea to another. Since God knows the content of his decree *in this manner,* the decretive act itself, reflecting this knowledge, is said also to be a single, simple act without parts or successive moments. As there is no mediation within God's knowledge, there is no mediation within the decree.

It is clear from this argument concerning the nature of God's knowledge, constructed to counter Arminian theology, that Reformed thought derives its understanding of the nature of the decree directly from the nature of God himself. And with this we move closer toward that absolute identification of the decree with God. The divine decree, as is clear in the theology of Francis Turretin, becomes divine in the absolute and unqualified sense in which God is divine.[4] Having been "incarnated" in the nature of God, the decree was frozen within the terms of the divine and eternal. And with this, decretal theology deprived itself of the category of God's freedom to move outside of himself in the historical—and into an incarnate Christ.

*   *   *

We have seen that scholastic Reformed theology maintains that the decree is single and simple, because God is a single and simple Being. This is the first step in the deification of the decree. We have also seen that since the decree is a divine idea, it must be single and simple, since God's way of

4 Locus IV, Question I, vii.

knowing is single and simple—that is, without parts or distinctions. This was a second step in the deification of the decree. We must now consider a third step in this deification.

Reformed theologians have insisted that the decree is eternal in the strict and absolute sense in which God is eternal. Berkhof asserts that while all of God's acts are "in a certain sense" eternal, we call those terminating in time not "eternal but temporal acts of God." The decree, however, "remains in itself an act within the Divine Being." It is "therefore eternal in the strictest sense of the word."[5] Hoeksema climaxes his discussion of the divine nature of the decree by asserting that "in a word, all the so-called incommunicable, as well as the communicable, attributes of God must be ascribed to the counsel of the living God."[6] Both men stand in the tradition of Turretin, who asserted in his polemic against the Socinians (who regarded God's decree as eternal only in a secondary sense), "We, however, believe that all the decrees are absolutely and simply eternal."[7]

The attribution of God's own kind of eternity to the decree has rarely been challenged in the Reformed tradition, despite the obvious element of confusion introduced by an assertion such as Berkhof's that all of God's works are "in a certain sense" eternal. Berkhof is merely reflecting the same confusion found in Turretin, who asserts that an imminent act of God "can be God absolutely," whereas such a divine work as creation "can be called God relatively."[8] Nothing, however, can be *relatively* God, and nothing can be eternal as God is eternal "*in a certain sense.*"

What is at issue here is obvious. These Reformed scholastics, whether of modern or seventeenth-century vintage, are struggling to articulate a meaningful biblical relationship between eternity and time. This effort was unsuccessful because they tried to relate eternity to time and time to eternity directly, the same way the ancient Greeks tried to relate them. But the eternality of God is no more eternally related

---

5 *Systematic Theology,* p. 104.

6 *Reformed Dogmatics,* p. 159.

7 Locus IV, Question II, i.

8 Locus IV, Question I, xv.

to time than time is temporally related to eternity. Between eternity and time lies God's act of creation. Hence God is not eternally related to time. Nor is God temporally related to eternity. Rather, as Thomas F. Torrance has pointed out, the eternal God who created time is *creatively* related to time.[9] Between eternity and time stands God's act of creation. This creative act, like God's re-creative act in Christ, is an expression of God's freedom. Decretal theology, however, never envisioned this. It tried to explain creation and re-creation—and, indeed, whatever comes to pass—in terms of the necessary essence of God, that is, in terms of what this necessary divine essence necessarily required and determined. It is characteristic of decretal theology to insist that the decree is divine and no less so than God himself. Nowhere is this argued more masterfully than in Turretin.

Turretin distinguished between three kinds of God's works. The first is that work by which the Father begets the Son, and Father and Son together spirate the Spirit. This work of God is wholly internal, intrinsic within God. Second is that work of God which occurs outside of himself—creation, providence, re-creation in Christ. Since these works occur outside of God, God is related to them extrinsically and bears no internal relationship toward them. It might seem that these two kinds of works cover the whole territory, but Turretin points to a third kind of divine work that bridges the gap between God's intrinsic and extrinsic works. This third kind of divine work is the decree.

Turretin is so far forth right: what God works both within himself and outside himself does indeed lie in God's decree, that is, in what God in his freedom decreed. Turretin, however, defines God's decree not in terms of his freedom but in terms of his own necessary essence and being. God's decree is as eternal, singular, and simple as God himself because, according to Turretin, the decree is a form of God's essence. The decree is God, and God is his decree. God could not be God without his decree, and the decree could not be other than it is because it is necessitated and determined by the very nature and essence of God's being. God and his decree

9 *Space, Time, and Incarnation,* pp. 10f.

are in the same sense eternal. "Scripture," says Turretin, "always speaks of eternity in the same manner."[10] Even if this claim is not true, Turretin has insured the unqualified eternality of the decree by identifying it with the essence of God.

How does God's decree exist in God? Turretin's answer employs the Greek concepts of essence or substance and accident. What makes a horse a horse in Greek thought? Its essence. The color of a horse, on the other hand, is an accident; for a horse is a horse whatever its color. According to Turretin, the decree exists in God *essentially,* not accidentally. It is of the essence of God. If the decree existed in God as something accidental, urges Turretin, it would be an "addition" and God could then not be a simple being. Furthermore, "the accidental is the root of all change, whereas God is immutable both in will and in essence."[11]

In what sense is God's will immutable? Turretin would not answer that God does not change his mind or that no man can alter the decree. His answer would be quite different. God's decree is immutable because it "is nothing other than his very essence willing." His will and decree are therefore "rightly said to be identical with his own essence."[12] If the decree is nothing other than the volitional form of God's essence, it must indeed be immutable and could in no sense be accidental, for the decree must be as immutable as the essence of God.

Turretin also thinks of the decree in terms of idea—that is, in terms of its content. In this sense, he says the decree is "nothing other than the divine essence itself, as it is known by God."[13] The decree, as the volition of God's essence, is simply God's self-knowledge of that essence. The decree as

10 Locus IV, Question II, v.

11 Locus IV, Question I, vi.

12 Locus IV, Question I, vii.

13 Locus IV, Question I, viii. T. F. Torrance says the idea was deeply intrenched in high medieval theology that "all created things have existence only as the objects of the eternal knowing and willing of God, so that their creaturely existence is directly grounded in the eternity of God." Although medieval scholastics did not accept the neo-Platonic idea that the world owes its reality to the overflow of the divine Being, it did hold to a modified view of the hierarchy

God's will is ontologically identical with God's essence, and as God's knowledge is ontologically identical with the divine self-knowledge of its own essence. In speaking of the decree as idea, Turretin can, therefore, use the phrase of the old scholastics and declare that "God is all." For if the decree is

of Being. What this "implied was an eternal positing or even co-existence of creaturely being with God's eternal Being which made it difficult to deny the *aeternitas mundi* [the eternality of the world]." Thomas Aquinas asserts in his *De aeternitas mundi contra murmurantes* that "there is no contradiction between affirming that something is created and that it never was non-existent." Torrance, quite rightly, regards this grounding of the world in God's Being as an undoing of the biblical doctrine of creation and of that divine grace and freedom of which creation is an expression.

What I am urging is that what St. Thomas said about creation and its eternality may rightly be said about God's decree, namely, that it is historical and yet eternal, that is, never was not. This allows the creation of the world to retain its biblical meaning as something once non-existent and, as an existent reality, to be an expression of God's freedom to be gracious.

Torrance also points out that high medieval scholasticism's tendency to regard nature, what is not-God, as grounded in God, even if in a graded hierarchy of Being, was an obstacle to the emergence of natural science. Combined with an appeal to the principle of causality, with its Aristotelian legacy of Nature as pervaded by Aristotle's Causes, scholastic theology hindered the rise of nature science. The study of nature could tell us little or nothing, for the pattern of nature is only an effect whose real truth lies in its Divine Cause (from which the effect, in neo-Platonic style, is but the emanation), that is, in its divine ground.

The way in which Turretin grounded God's decree in God's eternal essence, willing, and knowing does not essentially differ from the way medieval scholasticism viewed creation in terms of God's Being. As the scholastics regarded all creaturely existence as "directly grounded in the eternality of God" and therefore could not make a clear but only a blurred distinction between God and the world (one that threatened the biblical doctrine of creation), Turretin by grounding God's decree directly in God's essence was also unable to make a clear, unblurred distinction between what is God and what is not-God, that is, creation. This inability led him to assert that God's work of creation "can be called God relatively." But the assertion that creation is relatively God is simply an expression for a graded hierarchy of Being, and it forecloses the emergence and legitimacy of natural science as effectively as did high medieval scholasticism. Such a view of creation has the marks of paganism in which nature is worshipped but not subjected to scientific investigation and calculated experimentation.

The way in which Turretin understood God's decree reflects the way in which an earlier medieval scholasticism understood God's relationship to all created reality. Both the medieval and the later seventeenth-century Protestant (both Reformed and Lutheran) scholasticism were unable to understand that in biblical thought God's relationship to the created world lies in the biblical doctrine of creation in which God's creation of the world is not grounded in God's essence, or in its volitional and knowing function, but in his free and gracious decision to do what God was free not to do, create a world and by that act exercise his freedom to be gracious to what he created. For all quotations, see T. F. Torrance's *Theological Science*, pp. 59ff.

identical with God's essence, both as fact and content, without distinction, the phrase is appropriate indeed.

Clearly, Turretin identifies God's decree wholly with God himself, with his very being and essence. He must do this without qualifications, for nothing can be *partly* God. If the decree is a form of God's essence as will, idea, and act, and if "in God there is no difference between 'to be,' 'to be able,' and 'to act' since God does not act, as a creature does, through something added to his nature, but by his very essence,"[14] the decree is in fact God. In the strictest sense, then, it is eternal; indeed, all of God's attributes are to be ascribed to it.

This is the decree of decretal theology. Freedom is not an ingredient in it. God does not determine in freedom whether or not to have a decree, nor decide in freedom what its content is to be. God is no more free not to have a decree or to decree something other than he did, than he is free not to be God or to be some other kind of God than he is. To be God, according to decretal theology, God must have the decree he has, for the decree is itself God. One could say that God is stuck with his decree—though the decretal theologian would find such language irreverent, since he believes God's decree is identical with God's essence and thus with God himself. In decretal theology God is a decreeing God in terms of his ontology, not in terms of his freedom.

Such a view of the decree accounts for the tendency of scholastically oriented Reformed theologians to slip into the language of necessity. They can speak of a divine action as something God *had to do* because there were no other possibilities. They can slip into rationalism and make appeals to reason and logic to establish their view of the decree. Since they regard God as exhaustively rational, they regard the decree the same way. Thus it is open to rational demonstration.

What decretal theologians mean by divine sovereignty derives much of its connotation from this view of the decree. Decretal theologians, of course, do speak of God's sovereign freedom. Discussing God's speech to what is outside of him-

14 Locus IV, Question I, xv.

self, Hoeksema says, "It should be emphasized that this is not an act of necessity but of sovereignty, of sovereign freedom"—but then he continues: "determined by His sovereign, eternal counsel."[15] But what is a *"sovereign* freedom" that is *determined* by a *"sovereign* counsel"? It is no freedom at all. God's freedom is not determined by his counsel; his counsel is an expression of his freedom. Only on this understanding can we assert that God created and redeemed the world, not out of necessity, but in freedom, and that grace is an expression of God's freedom, not a necessary reflex according to which he is merciful to himself.

Turretin also speaks of God's freedom, but he defines it only after he has defined God's decree as identical with his essence, and then only within this equation of decree and essence. In what sense is God free according to Turretin?

> The freedom of the divine decree does not mean that it [the decree] is not God himself, because it [the decree] is free only from the standpoint of its object *[terminative]* and of the thing decreed; not subjectively or from the standpoint of God. It is free with regard to the act that is performed, in that the ability to decree either this or that resides in the freedom of God; but it is not free with regard to the act signified, because God's decreeing of anything depends on his own inner nature. The decree is free with regard to external relations, but not with regard to absolute existence in itself.[16]

In other words, the decree is free, not in the sense that it is other than God, nor in the sense that what is decreed is determined by something other than God's nature, but rather with regard to its external relations with the object decreed. Thus the decree is free *from* the world and its history. Nothing in the world and its history determines, affects, or conditions God's decree. Nothing in the decree, then, is of the nature of a free divine *response* to the realities of history. Everything outside of God and his decree is determined by God's own inner nature.

Consider what follows from this view. Election is not

15 *Reformed Dogmatics*, pp. 16, 17.
16 Locus IV, Question I, xiii.

God's free response to the plight of sinful fallen men. Wrath
is not God's free response to man's sin. Mercy and grace are
not God's free response (that is, a response that he in
freedom could have not made). Reprobation is not an act of
divine justice in response to sin. Compassion is not a free
response of God to the sufferings and misery of the sinner.
God is not *against* sin. Christ's triumph over sin and death
was not a triumph (for how can a God who decreed whatever comes to pass be against, much less triumph over, what
his essence decreed?).

Turretin's decree means that God is not free to *restrain*
sin through a general operation of the Holy Spirit, for such a
restraint of what God's own essential decree determined
would mean that he was working against himself. It also
means that nothing that occurs could be construed as an
antithetical, competitive force operating against God's decree. No man can oppose God's decree, for his seeming
opposition is itself an actualization of the decree. As A. C.
DeJong expressed it, "Man as creature together with all his
activities—in faith and unbelief—is never a competitor of
God."[17] How could any man be a competitor against, or an
enemy of God, if his very hostility is an actualization of that
divine decree which is an expression of God's own essence?

All these affirmations are a commentary on the nature of
God's freedom as understood by Turretin. Not only are God
and his decree conditioned by nothing lying outside of God;
what is more, God's decree is not an expression of his
freedom to respond—say in terms of election or reprobation,
grace or judgment—as he in his freedom freely relates to what
is outside himself. History, within the perspective of decretal
theology, is not a movement in which God has the priority
and initiative, and responds personally within this priority,
sovereignly, in grace and judgment, to the actions, whether
sinful or righteous, of human persons. On this view God does
not *answer* prayer, if by "answer" one means *responding* in
freedom or *reacting* to the cry of man.

This view of God's freedom as a freedom *from* the ter-
minal objects of his decree is the basis for Turretin's view of

17 *The Well-Meant Gospel Offer*, p. 80.

the relationship between God and what is outside of God. He contends that *God* does not change in relation to the world, because his relationship to the world is wholly external, extrinsic to him. The relationship changes, but God does not, since he is not in, or involved in the relationship. This profoundly impersonal view of God's relationship to man and his world is grounded in Turretin's belief that God and his decree determine whatever happens and that God, therefore, never becomes involved in the world and its history. This absolute form of unconditionality inherent in the decree of decretal theology requires that God's relationship to the world be wholly impersonal and uninvolved.

The basic weakness of decretal theology appears to be precisely its understanding of God's relationship to the world. If God is related to the world in terms of a decree that defines him in such a way that he is not personally involved in his relationship to the world, because such involvement would impinge on the unconditionality of the decree, then is God really related to the world at all? In any authentic understanding of God's relationship to the world, God is *in* the relationship and actually involved in what happens in the world. To be in relationship to anything means quite literally to be *in* the relationship. A "relationship" that is wholly external ("extrinsic," to use Turretin's word) is no relationship at all.

This does not mean that God can be conditioned and coerced by the world, or backed into a corner by sinful men. In creating the world and thereby relating himself to it God remained God, just as he did in becoming man in Christ. But when God *responded* to the sinful world in love and so loved the world that he gave his only begotten Son, in a profound way he related himself to, and became involved in, the world of his creation. Biblical thought portrays God as the Father of what he creates. This truth is reflected in the Apostles' Creed and in the various confessions of the church, for example, in the Heidelberg Catechism. In biblical thought God as father is always personally involved in what he fathered.

In creating the world, God conditioned himself, but with

this condition—that he remains God. God, in relating himself to that which is not-God, can be *in* his relationship to the world and yet remain God. It was rationalistic English Deism, not Christian theology, that understood God's creation of the world as the act of a cosmic clockmaker who makes a clock, winds it up, and then lets it run on its own.

The clue to God's decree is not to be found in the Greek distinction between essence (substance) and accident (that which is not necessary but contingent). Nor is it to be found in the Greek approach to eternity and time. It is to be found rather in the free act of God's creation and his re-creation in Christ. God's relationship to the world is neither that of his eternality in its relationship to time, nor of time in its relationship to eternity. The clue to the nature of God's relationship to the temporal world lies in his *creation* of a world of time. God *created* the time world, not by the necessity of his essence, not by an unfree and necessary decree, but in his freedom. Thereby he freely related himself to, and became involved in, his relationship to what he had freely created. God is neither temporally related to the world, for he created time; nor is he in the strict sense of his essential eternality related to the world, for his relationship to the world derives not from his necessary essence but from the free decision of his freedom. One asserts both of these things when one says that God is *creatively* related to the world, for God's act of creation means, in biblical thought, that God *in his freedom* created and *in this freedom* related himself in a personal and external relationship to the world.

The peculiar weakness of decretal theology appears in the fact that it has no room for transition, for movement, for a "history," for that *something* which cannot be derived from God's necessary essence, but by which he moves out of himself, without ceasing to be himself, into a personal and not merely external relationship to a world that is real by virtue of his free creative action. Decretal theology not only fails to include, but in fact excludes, a free and involved movement of God toward the world.

If this is the nature of God and his decree, how could God become man? How could Christ be the incarnate God, Immanuel, God-with-us in our death-ridden time and bloodstained history? Such a God is not the God of decretal theology who, in terms of his decree, can only be related to us in a manner wholly extrinsic and external to himself. That kind of divine relationship to the world excludes by definition God's presence and concern for the world in Christ. In terms of Turretin's definition of God's second kind of work, that is, his creation of the world, and God's purely external, extrinsic, impersonal relationship toward the world, how could God be personally present in the incarnate Christ? And in terms of Turretin's definition of God's essential decree, would not Christ himself be an illegitimate addition?

Turretin ascribes freedom to God, but it is a wholly negative freedom, a freedom *from* the world, not a freedom *for* the world. But in this kind of freedom, God is not free, for he can only decree what is necessary in terms of his own necessary essence and being. And such necessity does not include either the creation of the world or its re-creation in Jesus Christ. Christ is the free gift of God, the form in which God is free graciously to give himself to man. Such a free and gracious gift of himself falls wholly outside of any decree of God determined by the demands of his essence. This view of God and his decree and his relationship to the world can only be judged as profoundly unbiblical. Yet is not this essentially how Reformed thought came to regard the sovereignty of God?

God's sovereignty was regarded in Reformation thought as the sovereignty of his grace and of his judgment, that is, his freedom to be gracious or not to be gracious, to elect or not to elect. Sovereignty was freedom, understood in a positive sense as an internal, divine freedom in which God can, as it pleases him, relate to a sinful world in grace or in judgment or in both, in election or reprobation or in both, and, indeed, in his response of pity to the world's plight, can himself enter the world in Christ and go the way of the cross. God in Reformation thought possesses the internal freedom to love the sinful world and give his only Son for its redemption. The world cannot coerce God to do so, nor is he driven to do so by the necessity of his essence; if he had not in fact done so, he would not have violated a requirement of his essence. This is the crux of the Reformation phrase "salvation by grace," a grace that is free both in the sense that man by his works cannot claim it, and free in the sense that God in bestowing it does so in terms of his own internal freedom. As Jesus taught in the parable of the laborers in the vineyard, God has the right to do with his own as he wills.

But as this profound insight into the nature of God and his grace moved through the thought-processes of Reformed scholasticism, theologians came increasingly to speak of graceless divine sovereignty. Sovereignty was increasingly dissociated from grace and increasingly came to denote that God in his relationship to the world accounted for the *state* of the world, but did not in his freedom respond graciously to the world in its need. Supralapsarians insisted that God's redemptive action in Christ was not to be accounted for in terms of God's love, pity, and mercy for a fallen world, but in terms of the fact that God had himself willed that the world fall into its sinful and pitiful state. The infralapsarian position that God's redemptive action in Christ was a free and gracious divine response to man's pitiful condition was often discredited as redemptive "repair work," something far below the dignity of God. It was rejected as a form of Arminianism because it saw God as responding in freedom to man's sinful condition. This view was degraded as a form of *conditional* theology. Not only was conditional theology rejected in its Arminian version, according to which God's election is said to depend on man's meeting the condition of faith, but also in the sense of the assertions, "If you believe, God will save you," and "If you do not believe, God will damn you." Furthermore, conditional theology was rejected in the sense that reprobation was not to be regarded as the free response of God's justice to condemn the sinner for his sins, but in the sense that the basis of reprobation lies in God himself, not in the sinner's sin. God, it was sometimes said, is more glorified in the reprobation of the sinner to damnation, when the ground for it is seen to be in God and not in the sinner's sin.

What the Reformers meant by the sovereignty of grace— that is, God's freedom to be gracious to whom he will—came increasingly, as it developed in Reformed thought, to mean merely that God is free from any concern about the plight of the world, free in the sense of being unmoved by any moment within history. More and more, God was seen as accounting for whatever comes to pass in history, but not free to respond in grace to what occurs in history. He became like Aristotle's Unmoved Mover, who accounts for everything, but cannot respond in compassion to anything. He can only do what the decree (another name for his essence and will) requires. If all this is true, God did not and could not love the world in such manner as to give his Son to death for the sake of the world. He could only love the world and give his Son for *his own sake.* Which is only another way of saying that when God speaks to, loves, and is merciful and gracious to the world, he is really speaking to, loving, and being merciful and gracious to himself. Christ then did not die for the world, or did so only in a secondary sense; he died rather and primarily for God.

It is obvious that such a version of Christian truth cannot be preached. Imagine preaching to sinful men that Christ died for you; however, not *primarily* for you, but primarily and ultimately for God. Or that God loves you, but not you so much as himself. The kind of understanding of the gospel that is shaped and formulated by Turretin's understanding of God can only be properly preached to God himself. For if God in all his speech and gracious actions toward men is really speaking and being gracious to himself; if God's decretive actions are really the form in which God wills and thinks his own essence, then by the same token, God himself is the primary and most proper object of preaching. The God who can will nothing new is the object of the Good News! From the biblical standpoint this is absurd.

*   *   *

Turretin rejects causality as a concept that can be used to express God's relationship to his decree. Given his position, it is easy to see why. By definition, a cause is related to something other than itself, namely, to its effect. The concept of causality, therefore, does not illumine God's relationship to his decree, for God's decree (says Turretin) is identical with his essence, and God is God quite apart from any

relationship to something other than himself, that is, apart
from any relationship to what is not-God, namely, an effect.
God must not be regarded as the free *cause* of his decree,
since the decree is simply the necessary content of what his
essence necessarily wills, the necessary idea of God's knowledge of his own essence. A caused decree would have an
effect, and thus be an addition to God.

But if we were to ask Turretin how God is related to the
world and all that happens in it, his answer would be "causality." God is related to the world as a cause. Such a relationship is highly impersonal compared to the biblical terms
Creator, Father, Savior, Judge. Moreover, Turretin says that
God is the First Cause. As such, he determines everything
that is and everything that happens, yet in such a way that he
himself is not affected by anything that is or occurs in this
world.

How does God as First Cause accomplish all these external
works of creation and providence (including the provision of
man's redemption) without becoming personally involved?
By working through secondary causes. Everything that happens is decreed and must, therefore, necessarily happen.
Everything happens by necessity, for God as First Cause
determines its occurrence through secondary causes.

How helpful is this for a proper understanding of biblical
truth?

Let us consider Adam—the example that Turretin himself
used to illustrate his position. Turretin asks whether Adam
sinned by divine necessity. His answer is Yes. Did Adam sin
freely? His answer again is Yes. "It may be rightly said that
Adam sinned of necessity and in freedom."[18] In what sense,
then, was Adam's sin a free act and man's fall a contingent
act? In the sense that God as First Cause accomplished his
work through Adam as a secondary cause. Does this really
demonstrate that Adam possessed an authentic freedom?
Turretin says yes. He seeks support for his answer by ob-
serving that in created reality there are two kinds of
secondary causation. The first kind is necessary causation,
illustrated by fire, which *necessarily* burns. The second kind

18 Locus IV, Question IV, viii.

of secondary causation is free, contingent. Adam is the free agent through whom God effected Adam's sin and made its occurrence certain. The secondary causation that God employed to insure Adam's act of sin "could have been different."[19] God could have effected the event of sin through that other kind of secondary causation, says Turretin, the kind by which fire necessarily burns. This would be true, but only if God had made Adam a robot. Thus the best Turretin can do to demonstrate Adam's actual "freedom" in doing what God as First Cause determined he must do, is to say that God *might have used* the kind of necessary secondary causation by which fire necessarily burns. This argument is far from convincing unless one can believe that God could have made an Adam who would as necessarily sin as fire necessarily burns. The Bible presents us with neither such a God nor such an Adam.

The inadequacy of Turretin's effort is also apparent when he contends that the decree fixes the certainty of an event through secondary causation "but not [by] destroying the nature and properties of secondary causes." Astonishingly, Turretin again refers to Adam. When, as Turretin urges, God as the First Cause of sin determined its occurrence through Adam as a free secondary cause, were not the nature and properties of Adam as the secondary cause destroyed? Was not Adam broken by the event of the Fall? Did not he, and indeed all mankind, become enslaved to sin, fall under the divine curse, and become subject to death? Turretin's contention that "the decree does no violence to secondary causes" holds true for fire. Fire indeed necessarily burns—and it is none the worse for burning. But to make the same claim for Adam and the Fall is absurd.

Turretin's explanation of how God accomplished his decree to cause the event of sin in the world through secondary causes collapses at the crucial point, the point he himself selected to clarify his position.

The Westminster Confession also teaches this position. It too thinks of God as the First Cause of the eventuation in time of his eternal decree. God is said to "ordain whatsoever

19 Locus IV, Question IV, vi.

comes to pass." Then, in the same breath, thinking immediately of sin, the Confession adds "yet so as thereby neither is God the author of sin, nor is violence offered to the will of the creature, nor is the liberty or contingency of second causes taken away, but rather established" (III, 1). Here too we are told that, when God effected the Fall through Adam as a free secondary cause, Adam's reality as a secondary cause was thereby established! Either the Fall did not in fact occur, or God as First Cause wrought his work in and through Adam in such fashion that Adam and in him all mankind fell and freedom was indeed lost but not established.

The Synod of Dort, which convened in 1619, four years before Turretin was born and more than 25 years before the Westminster Assembly, did not speak of God as First Cause (nor of secondary causes), but specifically denied that God is the author of sin, designating that very thought as blasphemy. Indeed, the Canons explicitly assert that the cause and guilt of disbelief in Christ "as well as of all other sins *is no wise in God, but in man himself*" (I, 5). Reformed scholasticism had not yet reached the sophisticated point in its development where it could contend that God effected the event of the Fall through a secondary cause without destroying it (Adam), indeed in such manner as to establish its reality as a free and contingent cause.

In the endeavor to develop a theology of the single decree that would be as singular, simple, eternal, and unconditioned as is God himself, a theology that would account for sin, Reformed theologians recognized the problem of keeping God free from the authorship and guilt of sin. In trying to accomplish such a theology by the use of casuality, both primary and secondary, Reformed thought often urged quite self-consciously that God, though the First Cause of sin, is free from all taint of sin and that, as First Cause, God did not violate man as a free agent. The explanation of sin in terms of causality is obviously unsatisfactory. It is even more obviously unsatisfactory if we apply this scheme of causality, as Reformed theologians did not, as far as I know, to faith and salvation. If God is the First Cause and man the secondary cause of faith and salvation, then some credit for faith and salvation belongs to man as surely as the whole guilt of sin is said to belong to man. But by any Reformed standard such a view is Arminianism. In Reformed thought, man is not even the secondary cause of his faith and salvation. Reformed thought has always insisted that man is not saved *by* faith but *through* faith. To say the former might suggest that salvation is caused by faith; and so, the more precise theological formulation of "saved through faith" is preferred, in order to preserve for God alone the credit and glory.

If the causality scheme of Turretin and the Westminster Confession was an apt and useful way to conceptualize how God accomplished the will of his decree in human affairs, it should be most obviously apt and useful in the area of man's faith and salvation. But in this area it clearly distorts the very sovereignty of grace that was the main concern of the early Reformers. This alone calls for the rejection of causality as a serviceable theological concept. Even if some would want to retain it as the best available explanation of sin, it is still highly suspect, for it was projected by the exponents of God's single decree as a concept that throws light on how God effects in the world external to him the totality of that comprehensive decree which governs "whatsoever comes to pass."

Finally, causality as employed by Turretin again displays how profoundly impersonal God's external relationship to the world is thought to be. God is so little involved in his relationship to the world in all his external works that he can be the primary and ultimate cause of sin and yet bear no responsibility for it. Causality without responsibility. How mechanical and impersonal! And how, if not immoral, how amoral is God in all his works!

It seems clear that to maintain these positions is to lapse into verbalism, a theoretical game in which words really carry no ascertainable sense and phrases no ascertainable meaning. For it should be clear to all that causality does not mean the same thing in its application to God and to man. Something more distinguished than primary and secondary differentiates the divine and human causality, if the primal cause of sin carries no responsibility and the secondary causes carry all the responsibility.

If this critical evaluation leaves anyone unconvinced, let him consider that if God as the Primary Cause of sin is so uninvolved in it as to be wholly free of its guilt, then God as the Primary Cause of salvation is by the same understanding of causality also so uninvolved in it that he remains free of all the glory that the Bible affords him.

*   *   *

We have indicated what is meant by the single decree. On the basis of it Reformed decretal theology took its shape. Election and reprobation became so interrelated that the idea of the one can scarcely be distinguished from the other. Reprobation was seen as stemming from the logic of election, and it could be said that reprobation is the indispensable basis of election. It is on the basis of the single decree that election and reprobation are frequently defined by mere divine sovereignty, quite apart from man's sin or God's grace, or subsumed under a general doctrine of a predestination of whatever happens. Under the impact of the single decree without real distinctions, the peculiar qualities of both election and reprobation were largely blurred. Indeed, in the single decree lies the hidden but persistent motif that both threatens all human knowledge of God's decree, and at its deepest levels also threatens the actual reality of everything finite and historical. This explains Reformed theology's constant temptation to dissolve the historical character of Christianity in its search for eternal, timeless truth, and its persistent inclination to dismiss scriptural anthropomorphisms as insignificant accommodations to finite minds.

Finally, in the single decree lies the reason Reformed theology cannot absorb biblical eschatology and has not developed—and indeed cannot—a doctrine of the election of Israel, of the church, and of Jesus. Why not? Because the election of each of these denotes something special, distinctive, unique, as biblical eschatology denotes moments in time and history that are special, new, distinctive, and decisive in their impact on other historical moments. These distinctions of both election and eschatology cannot survive the impact of a single decree that governs all things, but filters out all distinctions because it is itself free of all distinctions and discrete moments. The deification of the divine decree that occurred in Reformed decretal theology cannot deal with the actualities of history, including those of biblical history. If the decree is divine because the one decreeing it is divine, and if the decree is no less divine than the one decreeing it, it has lost its applicability to historical reality. The single decree is a sheer irrelevant abstraction. Its advocates freely admit that what is most important about it—its singularity—cannot be known by the human mind.

Commitment to this single decree deprives Reformed theology of the freedom required for theological advance. It can only produce word games. A theology whose distinctive features are derived from the single decree is a theology whose distinctive features will not be preached. This regrettable situation has befallen most, if not all, Reformed churches. Election is one of Reformed theology's distinctive tenets, and it shapes numerous other distinctive Reformed doctrines. Yet election is hardly whispered in Reformed churches. And one rarely hears a sermon on its twin doctrine, the doctrine of grace. What is heard from Reformed pulpits in fact differs very little from what is heard in Arminian pulpits. The single decree that informs scholastic Reformed theology renders unpreachable every doctrine controlled and shaped by it.

Can the single decree and those doctrines determined by it be uttered in prayer? What Christian, confessing his sins before the face of God, would declare that he himself was only their secondary cause, and that God was their primary cause? No Christian would dare do so, for to pray in that way would be blasphemy. A theology that cannot be reflected in the language of prayer and worship is a theology that cannot be preached as something in which men should put their faith and trust.

Whatever a Christian authentically believes can be preached to others and in worship and prayer uttered before God. Under the dominance of the single decree of decretal theology, election is a doctrine that can neither be preached to the world, nor uttered before the altar of God in prayer and worship.

CHAPTER V

History, Eschatology, and God's Repentance

The gospel was not always true. The message the church proclaims is not an eternal, timeless truth, but an historical one. The gospel had to happen to become true. The gospel is the news of God's decision to be present and active in human history for man—more specifically, to be present and active in one man for mankind. This act of decision is God's election of Jesus to be the Christ for mankind. God was not always present and active in Jesus Christ. Because the election of Jesus Christ is, in a specifically historical sense of the word, eternal, it bears that event-character which characterizes the incarnation, birth, life, death, resurrection, and ascension of Jesus. If these events had not occurred, there would be no gospel. Because they did, the gospel is properly called news, good news. The church preaches a truth that happened. Christianity is in its very fabric an historical religion.

The event-character of the gospel must be stressed against existentialist theologians (like Bultmann) who regard it as something of minimum significance. What is decisive for them is not God's presence and action in history, but the decision of the individual through which he achieves authentic existence. Bultmann can dispense with the resurrection of Christ and settle for the idea that Christ becomes sufficiently alive in and through the preaching of the church to trigger in the hearer that decisive decision by which he attains authentic existence and becomes truly human.

This event-character of the gospel must also be urged upon Christian theologians of rationalistic bent. Such men think of the gospel as a body of timeless, eternal truth, historical only in the pale sense that it is in history that this timeless truth is revealed. They regard history not as the place where the gospel happened and became true, but as the mere medium in which an eternal truth became revealed. The historical is regarded as a kind of cosmic telephone, which conveys the eternal message, but is not part of it. This kind of rationalistic evangelicalism usually makes a strong defense of apologetics, insists on revelation as propositional truth, fails to appreciate the history and confessional traditions of the church, tends to value human decision in a manner not dissimilar to Bultmann, and is inclined to attach little value to symbol, sacrament, liturgy, and the dimension of mystery in the life of the church.

The point is neither that the gospel is irrational, nor that it is wholly closed to propositional statement. The point is that the kind of rationality that dissolves the event-character of the gospel is a rationalism foreign to the gospel. It would be folly, for example, to deny that Jesus' claim, "I am the way, the truth, and the life," is a proposition, but it is equal folly to theologize as though the ultimate form of that propositional truth is not the person and work of Jesus Christ. For Christ is the way, truth, and life precisely because his birth and life occurred. The way, truth, and life is what Christ *became.*

The event-character of the gospel must also be stressed against a theology that is grounded and shaped in the idea of the single decree. Decretal theology has always had difficulty with the event-character of Christianity. This is reflected in the trouble Reformed theology has always had with history.

The German philosopher and dramatist Gotthold Ephraim Lessing (1729-1781) raised a crucial question about Christianity. Christianity claims to be an historical religion, inextricably bound up with Jesus of Nazareth. It also claims finality for its truth. Given its peculiar character as an historical religion how, asks Lessing, can it claim finality for itself? An eternal truth, he urged, cannot be contingent on a temporal event: a necessary truth cannot depend on an accidental, that is, historical datum. A necessary truth *is;* it is therefore eternal. Christian truth *became;* it is therefore neither eternal, absolute, nor necessary.

History is a matter of occurrence, and it is of the nature of the historical that it might not have occurred. In contrast to an eternal truth that necessarily is, historical truth always contains the ingredient of freedom. It must be recognized that Lessing raised a fundamental question when he asked how Christianity as an historical religion could claim to be a final, absolute truth. Christian theology cannot afford to ignore the challenge of Lessing's question.

Lessing's answer to his own question was that since Christian truth is an accidental, historical truth, a truth that might not have happened, it lacks the quality of a necessary, eternal, absolute truth. *From his own perspective,* he gave the right answer. For he defined eternal, absolute truth in terms of the ontologically necessary, just as decretal theologians defined God's decree (the truth of all reality) in terms of God's essential being.

But if Christian truth is ontologically identifiable with God, it loses its historical character. God is eternal and necessary; as he is in himself he is not marked by that contingency which characterizes the historical. God is not an occurrence, a reality that might not have been. God necessarily is. If Christianity is an historical religion, its truth is not *ontologically* necessary; if its truth is ontologically identical with God, its truth is not an historical truth and Christianity is not an historical religion. Within the presuppositions of both Lessing and decretal theology, Christianity cannot be both historical and eternal, accidental and necessary, contingent and absolute, a phenomenon that necessarily happened and also one that might not have happened.

Lessing's rejection of Christianity as final truth was not a live option for decretal theologians. Yet for all their Christian commitment, their inability to give the historical its rightful place and function, as is amply evident from their theology, indicates their inability to understand Christian truth as both eternal and historical.

But Lessing's problem disappears, as does decretal theology's inability to grant the historical its rightful place, if it is

recognized that the reality of Christian truth as both historical and final arises out of the freedom of God. In this
freedom God decrees his decree; in this freedom God creates
a world; in this freedom God redeems a fallen world. The
exercise of this divine freedom possesses the character of the
historical and is an expression of it.

In his freedom God decreed. As an unnecessary decree, as
a decree that bears the pedigree of the historical, it might not
have been. There is a gap between the reality of God as he
necessarily is and the reality of the decree. This gap is
traversed by God's freedom. The movement between God
and his decree is the unnecessary divine act of decreeing.
Such an eternal act, arising out of God's freedom, bears the
mark of the historical as that which might not have been. But
as an act of divine freedom that did indeed occur, the act is
constituted by that combination which Lessing thought impossible, and decretal theology within its presuppositions
could not acknowledge: a combination of the historical and
the eternal.

One may indeed, therefore, speak of the eternal, absolute
finality of Christian truth, provided he says these things
within the context of God's freedom and does not regard
them as derived from the nature and being of God. Lessing
could not conceive a truth both absolute and historical. To
attempt to do so in terms of God's necessary nature, as he
did, and as decretal theologians do, is a contradiction in
terms. The concept of the historical cannot be simply related
to God's necessary eternality. God is not an historical God.
He is not (process theology to the contrary) in process.
Hence the concept of God as he is in himself cannot be
meaningfully combined with the concept of history. But
Christianity can intelligibly be regarded as both historical and
final (eternal, absolute) when its truth is seen as deriving
from the freedom of God. God's decree is both eternal and
event, and both as an eternal act of his freedom. As such, what
God decreed is both absolute *and* historical, historical both as
an event in God and as actualized in the world external to God.
Thus understood, the free decision of God's decree bridges
Lessing's gap between the eternal and the historical.

To say that Christian truth is defined in terms of God's

freedom does not contradict the nature of God. For God became historical in the same way he became incarnate. As he became man without ceasing to be God, he became historical without ceasing to be eternal. Note that these are not two parallel affirmations; they are two affirmations about the same event. What God did in Christ was to become man and thereby to become historical. This action did not derive necessarily from his nature, nor did it occur in contradiction to it; it was an event of his freedom. In this sense Christian truth is an event, a truth both historical and absolute. God's becoming man, historical, is something too large for us to comprehend fully, but it is not wholly unintelligible. The way Lessing posed the problem, however, foreclosed the possibility of understanding Christianity as being both historical and final. And the way decretal theology ontologically identified the single decree with God foreclosed the possibility that it could take history seriously.[1]

*   *   *

One of the characteristics of human history is conflict. History is a moving stream, sometimes tranquil but often turbulent and violent, with many currents running within and against each other. History contains contradictions. Forces and counterforces often crash in convulsive upheavals and threatening crises. History is creative and destructive; it builds and it tears down. When the errors of the past catch up with the present, history is precipitated into crisis and comes under its own judgment. Even individual human life is filled with ups and downs, anxieties and frustrations, hope and despair, achievements and setbacks. What human history and life would be like without conflict we cannot even imagine.

Decretal theology cannot deal with historical conflict. If true to itself, it cannot even recognize historical conflict. Viewed from the perspective of decretal theology, each event of history is willed by God, is related vertically to the divine determination, and is revelatory of the divine glory. This is

[1] The peculiar character of the historical is that what happens might not have happened. The peculiar character of divine grace, similarly, lies in the fact that grace bestowed might not have been bestowed. Indeed, this "might not have been" characterizes every divine act and work that arises out of God's freedom.

God's sovereignty. Theologians in this tradition urge that God is the ultimate cause and the primary source of sin, that the function of the proclamation of the gospel is to make some men ripe for judgment; that God created sin (Gordon Clark);[2] that God takes pleasure in the death of sinners; that preaching is *per se* a curse for the reprobate; that everything that occurs is a divine wish-fulfilment, for if anything were to occur contrary to what God wills, God would not be sovereign but a godling who had created more world than he can take care of (B. B. Warfield).[3] Such theological assertions cannot be dismissed as enthusiastic and excessive overstatements or written off as putting too much emphasis on God's sovereignty. On the contrary, such statements simply articulate the inherent theology of the single decree. Those who make such assertions understand the theology of the single decree better than those who discount their formulations as excesses.

According to the thoroughgoing decretal theologian, there cannot be irrationalities in history, for everything that happens is in God's decree, which all regard as a true reflection of the divine essence, if not identical with it. Surely God is not irrational in any of his ways and works! Since God wills whatever comes to pass, all that comes to pass is rational, wholly without irrational elements or conflicting moments. Cornelius Van Til finds Hegel's assertion that "the rational is the real and the real is rational" completely acceptable if defined in a Christian context. He also holds that reality contains no irrationalities. Van Til does, however, admit the existence of the immoral in history, which he resolves by asserting that God is the primary and man the secondary cause of moral evil. But he is unwilling to grant the existence of irrationalities in history and to resolve them by regarding God as their primary and man as their secondary cause. Why? First, because he believes that God—and therefore also God's decree—is exhaustively rational, that is, wholly definable in terms of rationality. Second, if he regarded irrationalities as

---

[2] "The Bible therefore explicitly teaches that God created sin." *Biblical Predestination*, p. 12.

[3] *Selected Shorter Writings of Benjamin B. Warfield*, I, 103.

he regards moral evil, he would lose the foundation for his particular kind of apologetics, whose distinctive feature is that nothing has meaning apart from God's decree, and everything is meaningful and rational in terms of it.

But would it be more difficult for decretal theology to maintain God's rationality if it held that he actually did will irrationalities, than it is for decretal theology to maintain the moral character of a God who is said to have willed sin? The answer is No. Decretal theology is very vulnerable in its inability to maintain the gravity of sin. If God is the ultimate cause of sin, his love for the world, his gift of his Son, and Christ's death on the cross lose their absolute and utter seriousness; and the ultimate revelation of God's sovereignty and glory lies as much in God's causation of sin as in his triumph over it. This of course renders the triumph suspect.

Decretal theology ignores this problem. It simply asserts that the God who is the ultimate cause and source of sin is not the author of sin. Why the ultimate cause and source is not its ultimate author or even its secondary author, and how there can be ultimate causation of sin without any responsibility, are not explained.

Does history contain contradictions? Is one moment of history in conflict with another? Again the answer of decretal theology is negative. History can no more be in conflict with itself than can God's essence. God wills every item of history; history is an actualization in time and space of the will of his decree. Since the decree is identical with, or at least a pure reflection of, his essence, history cannot contain contradictions. A decree and a history that contained internal conflicts would be irrational.

We finite creatures do speak of historical contradictions, however. If we understand decretal theology and are loyal to it, we qualify such speech and assert that these are only "apparent contradictions." We use the term "contradiction" to describe what we see and experience. But if we are loyal to the heritage of decretal theology, we admit that when we speak of such contradictions we are thinking about history within the limitations of finite thought. If we could see history as it is willed by God's essence, we too could see that history contains no contradictions, conflicts, irrationality. We would acknowledge that this is merely the way things appear to finite, limited minds, that the contradictions and conflicts we experience, contend with, agonize over, and pray about every day are not real at all. Since we do not experience life in this way, we must live by faith. If we live by faith, not by what we see nor by the insights of the finite mind, we acknowledge that human life is a simple and beautiful harmony. We gladly acknowledge that the clash of historical forces, contention between economic systems, racial groups, warring nations, all the explosive convulsions, upheavals, and crises in the personal and social life of man, all the demonic cruelties of history, all the storm and stress, all the shouting and tumult, all are in reality a beautiful harmony, a divinely woven artistic pattern, each thread in place.

Decretal theology is a profound rationalization of whatever is. Like all rationalization, it reduces reality to harmony, proportion, symmetry, unity. All reality reflects the unbroken beauty of the divine essence. With his eye of faith the decretal theologian can look out on a broken, bleeding humanity, on a world at war with itself, and see only a thing of beauty and peace. Let us try to concretize this by two examples.

In 1968, when Senator Robert Kennedy was assassinated in Los Angeles, the world was numbed with grief and horror. A decretal theologian true to this theological commitment would have to respond to this deed by asserting that "it is God's will," and would speak of the beautiful harmony of the will of God that had decreed it. To be sure, at the close of Kennedy's funeral service, St. Patrick's Cathedral echoed with the music of Handel and the majestic words, "The Lord God Omnipotent reigneth, and He shall live forever and ever." But these words were sung not as a commentary on the assassination, but as a cry of faith against it!

During the bloody days of the Civil War, Julia Ward Beecher was in the Willard Hotel in the heart of Washington, D.C. Looking out of her window one night she was struck by all the realities of war she saw outside. Through the dark of the evening she saw the lights of the camps surrounding the city. She wrote what she saw in what we know as the *Battle Hymn of the Republic*. What her eyes saw through her hotel window that night were all the brutalities and conflict and violence that was the American Civil War. But her Christian faith saw more. She declared, "Mine eyes have seen the glory of the coming of the Lord." She saw his day and his truth marching on.

Julia Ward Beecher was no decretal theologian. From the Willard Hotel that night, she did not see the Civil War as itself the will, the glory, the truth, or the day of the Lord. In the horror of that war she did not see the Lord, but the *coming of the Lord;* not the Day of the Lord, but the day of *the Lord marching on.* She saw the glory of the Lord not in the Civil War, but in the fact that God through that war was "trampling out the vintage where the grapes of wrath are stored." God was doing his work of judgment, moving toward his divine purpose. The war was not God's glory, but a day when God's truth was marching toward its glory. In short, she saw the Civil War eschatologically, as a movement of the Lord through judgment toward the attainment of his truth and glory.

A decretal theologian could not have written the *Battle Hymn of the Republic.*[4] Had he looked out from the Willard Hotel that night he could only have declared that what his eyes saw was itself the will of the Lord, a reflection of the essence of God, the externalization of what God in his essence willed, and the external content of God's internal self-knowledge. The *Battle Hymn of the Republic* is a doxology. In biblical thought, a doxology is the music and language of the final outcome. And what Julia Ward Beecher wrote while looking out over Washington during the Civil War was oriented in terms of the future as seen under God. Decretal theologians, on the other hand, do not write doxologies, because decretal theology ends where it begins—with one foot in heaven and the other in hell.

In short, whenever decretal theology is matched with his-

---

[4] Warfield, for example, said about the well-known hymn that says, "I was a wandering sheep—I would not be controlled," that this last sentence would be theologically accurate if it asserted that "we will not admit that we are controlled." The "wandering" that this hymn confesses as a sin, in Warfield becomes something determined by God, and the sin is not that of wandering from the fold, but the refusal to admit that our sinful wanderings occurred because of God's control. *Ibid.,* p. 103.

tory, it appears tragically unrelated to the facts of life. The Civil War was no concert of harmony, no aesthetic datum. And no rationalistically contrived definition will convince anyone, except those who traffic in theological abstractions, that the Civil War was a divine wish-fulfilment, a design of divine harmony—if we only had better-than-finite vision we would see that an apparent historical conflict was in fact a thing of beauty reflecting the nature of God's singular will and the serenity of his essential being.

Decretal theology denies not only all contradictions and disharmonies in the data of history. It also denies that anything in history can go contrary to God's decree. The counsel of God is such that nothing can contradict it, for the very contradictions are themselves willed by the decree, and are, therefore, only apparent and seeming contradictions of the decree. Luke speaks of publicans who "justified God, having been baptized with the baptism of John," and he speaks also, in contrast, of "the Pharisees and the lawyers [who] rejected the purpose of God for themselves, not having been baptized by him" (Luke 7:29, 30). Luke is saying that these latter reject the counsel of God. But decretal theologians cannot—and do not—allow these words to have their force. Turretin alludes to this text and argues that it does not teach a conditional decree. This is true. But it is also beside the point. The counsel of God in this passage, says Turretin, does not mean God's decree but his will in a commandment. God, he says, commanded the Pharisees through the preaching of John to be baptized and they refused. What they refused, he urges, was not the counsel of God's decree. The decree, in the definition of decretal theology, cannot be rejected.

In biblical thought, what can be preached may be believed or rejected. But the decree, according to decretal theology, cannot be rejected. Hence Turretin, in defense of his decretal theology, is compelled to take Luke's affirmation that by rejecting John's baptism the scribes and Pharisees rejected the counsel of God and declare that here God's counsel is merely God's command. If it were indeed God's counsel, urges Turretin, it could not be rejected. But if so, then the counsel of God cannot be preached, for what can be preached can be accepted *or* rejected. Yet no one urges more

than decretal theologians the necessity of preaching the
"whole counsel of God." But the decree as they define it
cannot be preached (which is one of the major theses of this
book). Turretin's exegesis, however, also illustrates a more
immediate concern, namely, that decretal theology cannot
recognize historical resistance against the single decree.

On the other side, decretal theology also excludes divine
resistance against history. Since all things are viewed as willed
by God, God does not resist what he has willed. Hoeksema
rejected the existence of a general operation of the Spirit in
history. The Spirit, he held, neither resists the evil inclina-
tions of the human heart (restraint of sin), nor resists the
nature of the sinner by enabling him in his actual conduct to
be better than he is by his nature (civic righteousness).
Although most Reformed theologians do not agree with
Hoeksema, his rejection of a general operation of the Spirit is
wholly in agreement with decretal theology's understanding
of the single decree.

Thus decretal theology, when true to itself, denies that
there is any real resistance or conflict (a) between the data of
history, (b) between history and God, and (c) between God
and history. In none of the dimensions of historical interaction between God and man is there real conflict. On the
contrary, the whole is seen as an ordered logical system.
Every relationship is serenely intact; every item is perfectly
placed in the grand design.[5] This is how history would appear
to us, it is said, if we could see it as God sees it. Since we are
not God, of course, but only finite minds, we see historical
conflicts, resistance, and antitheses everywhere. And it is
only legitimate, we are told, to see history as we do if (as
Berkhof says) we remember that things are not as they
appear to our time-conditioned way of thinking.

But place this bloodless decretal version of history alongside the history given in the pages of the Bible. Now anguish
displaces the aesthetic mood. All similarity vanishes. In the
biblical record, Israel's history is a long story of conflicting

[5] When Hoeksema describes human life, he speaks of "friction, conflict,
death, destruction," but also of "*apparent* foolishness." *Reformed Dogmatics*, p.
46. Even when conflict is recognized, the total rationality of history is maintained.

movements, times of crisis, days of judgment. Israel rebels against God, resists his grace, denies the covenant, serves idols, walks in the way of paganism, distorts her election. God responds in judgment, moves nations to war against her, hides his face, withdraws his presence and blessing. Because Israel sins, "the Lord has a controversy with his people, and he will contend with Israel" (Micah 6:2). Israel repents and returns to Yahweh, and he again causes his face to shine upon them. Israel's whole troubled history is one of resistance against and a return to Yahweh, of action and interaction between Israel and God in blessing and judgment.

All this suggests nothing of a single decree which determines all, but is itself free of conflict, serene as the divine being itself. Is it possible to read the history of Israel and hold that all its troubled conflict is only the way things appear to finite minds?

Or consider the New Testament. Are we to believe that Jesus as the sign of contradiction that shall be spoken against, his temptations, the rejection of the Christ, his contest with and victory over the demonic powers of darkness, sin, and death, the triumphant character of the Resurrection, the tension between Jew and Greek—are we to believe that all these are moments and events of only apparent conflict and triumph, moments that, if seen from the perspective of the Eternal, are things of aesthetic beauty, data of tranquil design and divine artistry?

The point is not that God cannot or does not bring order out of chaos, good out of evil, light out of darkness, life out of death. He does. The point is that God *brings* light out of darkness, *turns* death into life, and *creates* beauty out of chaos. But these are acts of divine *accomplishment*. Life and death, war and peace, chaos and beauty are not decreed by God in the same manner, so that there is no distinction except that which appears before finite minds. And precisely because God does not will these things "in the same manner," he can use the worse to achieve the better and in the process eliminate the worse. Through death Christ overcame death and displaced death by the Resurrection.

Reformed theologians often speak of seeing things from the "viewpoint of eternity" (*sub specie aeternitatis*), and from the "human point of view," that is, from "the perspective of history." There is no objection *per se* to these distinctions. Our seeing and knowing are finite and not identical with God's seeing and knowing. But it is another thing to use such distinctions under the impact of decretal theology to preserve that kind of version of the divine decree which is without moments or items of conflict. By making the single decree as eternal and divine as God (to say nothing of making it identical with the necessary rational volition of the divine essence), decretal theology deprives itself of ever getting a handle on history. The possibility of taking history seriously, as real and not merely apparent, is foreclosed by the scholastic definition of the single decree.

*   *   *

All history in biblical thought is eschatological. Like an arrow shot toward a mark, history moves toward a goal. It is teleological in two senses: it has a goal and an end. When it reaches its goal, it will also have arrived at its end. What follows that, in biblical idiom, is the eternal sabbath.

But the movement of history toward its goal is not one of steady, even progression. Rather, history moves unevenly, with advances and setbacks, triumphs and defeats. Time does not as such measure history's approximation to its goal. Each day does not make an equal contribution: some are more decisive than others. This fact is an inherent feature of biblical eschatology. It is reflected in biblical phrases like the "day of the Lord," the "year of the Lord," the "fulness of time"; in references to a nation's "cup of iniquity being filled"; and in the distinctive significance the Bible attributes to the "old" and the "new," for example, the *Old* and *New* Testaments, the *new* commandment, the *new* covenant, the *new* song. It is reflected in the cross as an "end of the ages" event and the Resurrection as the "new eon."

The significance of old and new in the Bible is not one of mere temporal succession. The new is significant not only because it comes later on the time line. If history does not move an equal distance each day toward its goal, neither does it move toward its goal through a steady process of temporal accumulation. Biblical eschatology is more complex than such a simplistic view would suggest. This is evident in the meaning of Christ's lordship over all time, which demonstrates that the biblical eschatological moment can transform the past and no less determine the future. A later moment can render new a past old and determine the future in terms of that new. To illustrate, the New Testament, though it is not new apart from the old, is a new form of the old. Moreover, the new of the New Testament is also a moment of such decisiveness that it can, so to speak, determine in advance the future in terms of the new.

For all the difficulties biblical eschatology presents for our thought, it is obvious that it rejects the notion that each moment of time is equally significant and holds that one moment can be decisive for—and so more significant than—others, whether earlier or later on the time line. A moment can both fulfil earlier moments and be the fulness of later moments. A moment can annul a prior moment, as occurs in the forgiveness of sins, an annulment so effective that Scripture can speak of God as "remembering our sins no more." A moment can exclude from the future the return of a prior moment, as is asserted in the nature of Christ's death as a once-for-all event, and in Revelation's depiction of the new Jerusalem as having no more night and no more tears. Events like these cannot recur, because of their decisive quality.

The primal eschatological moment is that of the life, death, and resurrection of Jesus Christ. This moment divides history decisively into B.C. and A.D., a division of time that cannot be repeated or altered. This moment is absolutely decisive; it gathers all the past and all the future into itself so profoundly and mysteriously that the end and goal of history are in a real sense present in Christ as the Alpha and the Omega, the first and the last.

Defined by decretal theology in terms of its single decree, history cannot grasp this distinctive complexity of biblical eschatology. The decretal theologian, who sees the single decree as without distinguishable moments, can only regard each moment and each event as equally willed by God and therefore neither more nor less decisive than any other moment. Since he conceives the decree rationally, he cannot consider any historical datum as more related logically to one moment than to another. Logical relationships between the data of history can only be rational or irrational, serene or turbulent; they cannot be partial or relative. But time is partial and relative, and succession is the nature of time. And it is precisely this distinction between moments, which lies in the biblical eschatological understanding that one event can be more decisive than another, that is completely absent in decretal theology's understanding of history and, particularly, biblical eschatology.

Decretal theology flattens the time line, rendering every event equally significant and thereby excluding the possibility of a moment of special significance and decisive power. Since God wills everything in the same manner, everything is equally meaningful.

This "in the same manner" is so characteristic of decretal theology's single decree that serious consideration of biblical eschatology falls wholly outside its grasp. That is why Reformed theology has traditionally been unable to relate biblical history and theology. That is why Reformed theology has always been weak in biblical theology, in sharp contrast to its genius for systematic theology. That is why eschatology is an undeveloped locus of Reformed systematic thought (which takes eschatology to be the category of end-time and end-time events, rather than something under the lordship of Christ). That is why Reformed theology fails to take seriously the historical aspects of Paul's theology of Jew and Gentile in Romans 9-11. That is why Reformed theology has never as much as attempted to develop an historical doctrine of election, but has remained content with a purely ahistorical doctrine of individual election. Finally, that is why the mystery Paul sees in the election of the Gentiles, of Christ, and of the church is almost totally absent in Reformed thought. Rationalism flattens out all moments and events into data of equal meaning and significance and thereby evaporates all mystery. There is no mystery in a syllogism. Reformed churches generally have no deep feel for Paul's profound sense of the mystery of Christ and his church.

Before we leave this discussion about the biblical eschatological moment, we should take a further look at decretal theology's rejection of the "decisive moment." Decretal theology relates each moment to God's decree in vertical directness. Were it to recognize the validity of the distinctive eschatological moment, whose power fulfils or annuls another moment, it could see that in God's decree (or, if you will, in the actualization of his decretive will in history) one moment can be *conditioned by* another moment. But if one moment conditions another moment, God's decree would at such a point reflect its decisiveness over other moments. The decree itself would then become historically involved in history. Decretal theology would regard this (as Hoeksema contended) as a form of conditional theology that impairs God's absolute sovereignty and the total determination of his decretive will. Berkhof reflects the same antipathy for this kind of conditional theology in his discussion of infralapsarianism. "Infralapsarianism really wants to explain reprobation as an act of God's justice. It is inclined to deny either explicitly or implicitly that it [reprobation] is an act of the mere good pleasure of God." Berkhof then gives his evaluation of the infralapsarian denial of reprobation as an act of God's "mere good pleasure." This, he says, "really makes the decree of reprobation a conditional decree" and "leads into the Arminian fold."[6]

If the moment of reprobation is a response of God's justice to man's sin, and not an act of the *mere* good pleasure of God, then the moment of reprobation is a divine *response* to the moment of man's sin, and God's act of reprobation depends on the reality of man's sin. This, says Berkhof, is conditional theology, and this road leads to Arminianism. If one moment of God's decree is conditional and hence responsive to another moment in the decree, if one divine act in history is conditioned by, and responsive to, another divine act in history, if man's sin is *in any sense or degree* the basis for reprobation and the occasion for an act of divine justice, decretal theology loses the distinctive basis on which it rests. The infralapsarian—or anyone else who thinks reprobation is in any degree conditional—is said to forsake the distinctive core of the Reformed faith. This peculiar view of decretal

6 *Systematic Theology*, p. 123.

theologians is grounded in the tenet that no moment in God's decree can be determined by, nor determinative of, another moment. But the reality of such decisive moments belongs to the very essence of biblical eschatology.

*   *   *

There are many statements in the Bible which speak about God in human terms—anthropomorphisms (from Greek *anthropos,* man, and *morphe,* form) they are often called. When the Bible speaks of God as having eyes and looking down from heaven, the assertion is anthropomorphic; God is spoken of in human terms.

Since the supreme revelation of God comes in terms of a man, Jesus Christ, since the word of God as Scripture is a divine word in terms of human language and, further, since all God's revelation occurs in history, the question may well arise whether all divine revelation does not in fact appear in human, finite, historical form. This is a rich question with an obviously clear answer, but we cannot pursue it here. Decretal theologians have had a special interest only in a certain class of biblical anthropomorphisms, those which say something about internal divine responses to external realities.

When the men of Nineveh repent, is it really true (and this puts it prejudicially, because there is no other way to put it) that "God repented of the evil which he had said he would do to them, and he did not do it" (Jonah 3:10)? Is it possible for a man to do something that can "grieve the Holy Spirit" (Eph. 4:30)? When Jesus wept at the grave of Lazarus (John 11:35), over Jerusalem (Luke 19:41), in Gethsemane (Heb. 5:7), were these merely human tears, revealing nothing of God? When God cries, "When Israel was a child, I loved him, and out of Egypt I called my son. . . . How can I give you up, O Ephraim! How can I hand you over, O Israel! How can I make you like Admah? How can I treat you like Zeboiim? My heart recoils within me, my compassion grows warm and tender" (Hosea 11:1, 8), are we really hearing sounds of a rending divine pathos, the yearning of a hurt love?

Decretal theology's answer to all these questions is No. All these are said to be merely finite, human ways of speaking about God. They no more point to such data within God than the multiplicity of distinguishable items and moments of finite history point to such distinctions within the single decree. The nature of the single decree dictates that statements about God's interior life be reduced to the limitation of the finite mind, which is really to say to the limitations of the *historical.* Thus in decretal theology God is not free to move out of himself into the world, nor is anything historical, via that divine freedom, able to affect God's life. Accordingly, decretal theology also supports its negative answer by pointing to the way in which God is related to the world. God, as we have seen, is not considered to be *personally* involved in his relationship to the world, hence he is not personally affected by what occurs in the world. God was not free to be moved by Nineveh's repentance of its sin and to repent of his promised judgment. Nothing in the world can affect God.

This whole matter is contained in the decretal theologian's doctrine of the immutability of God. If God were free to be affected by anything in the world, if he were moved, say, by the sinner's plight, he would then experience some internal personal movement or change. A God who could change would not be a sovereign God. God can create, redeem, change and move the world, but he remains himself unmoved. To use Aristotle's term, God is the Unmoved Mover.

Like every kind of Reformed theology, decretal theology does not want a God who is unreliable or subject to man's whims. Nonetheless, one must consider whether the theological ground on which any theology protects itself against such a God-in-the-hands-of-man is solid. The question must be asked of decretal theology because of the plight into which anthropomorphisms are abandoned by its position. If ascribing repentance to God is merely a human way of speaking and does not mean that God actually repents, *what* is being said when it is asserted that God repents? Unless we come to terms with this, how shall we retain the profound truth and comfort of the Pauline statement that "the gifts and the call of God are irrevocable [that is, *not* repented of]." Decretal theology gives us no answer. It simply insists that God cannot repent. But that is not enough.

The theological ground for the decretal theologian's negative answer threatens some very basic Christian concepts. God has been protected against internal change, but on grounds that threaten such concepts as grace, love, and mercy. Decretal theologians have not hesitated to insist that God's love for man is really God's love for himself. God, it is said, loves his own image in man.

There is an element of truth in this. It would be folly to claim that God does not love—or even hates—man as an image of himself. But unless one is cautious at this point one can easily lose both the reality of the divine love and the reality of man himself. Man is no mere narcissistic reflection of God. Man is indeed made in the image of God; but to the extent that the creation is real and authentic and not merely apparent or seeming, man is real and what God loves in loving man is not merely himself, but man. Furthermore, to the extent that God's love for man is defined as self-love, to that extent the Christian concept of divine love is lost. Here again we see that the rationalistic feature of decretal theology throws a threatening shadow over the reality of creation and over the reality of divine love.

The solution decretal theology offers is too simple. In biblical thought, God loves the sinner, not because, but *even though* he is a sinner. Paul says "God shows his love for us in that while we were yet sinners Christ died for us" (Rom. 5:8). The historical dimension of the "while" must be recognized. But it must also be recognized that the object of God's love is not merely man as the self-reflection of God. In his reality as sinner, man is not that. But the object of the divine love is precisely sinful man; and God's love is shown, Paul says, in the consideration that Christ died for man *while* a sinner. When decretal theology develops a position that does not just permit but requires that the concept of divine love be so defined that the reality of the divine love and its object begin to evaporate, it is obvious that this basic position is far from acceptable.

Hoeksema, it will be recalled, denies that there is a divine love for sinners. God, he contends, hates sinners and loves the righteous because they are, in Christ, *righteous*. Furthermore, we have seen that Hoeksema also held some other strange positions: that in speaking to man God speaks primarily to himself, and that in being gracious, merciful, and longsuffering with man, God is primarily being gracious, merciful, and longsuffering with himself. Hoeksema fortifies this position by contending that God *is* gracious, merciful, and longsuffering *to himself*. Not all decretal theologians go this far, but in fact Hoeksema is only being consistent with the basic motif in terms of which decretal theologians generally interpret those biblical anthropomorphic assertions that speak of divine repentance.

No reality in time or history, according to decretal theology, affects God. Nor is God even free to allow himself to be affected. God is absolute and unconditioned. For this reason none of the distinctions of historical data or temporal moments characterize the single decree.

These views of God have been so developed in decretal theology that all reality—man, history, divine love, grace, mercy—is threatened. Critics of decretal theology have often been charged by decretal theologians with surrendering God's sovereignty and his immutability. But in decretal theology all created and redemptive realities tend to evaporate.

But do the Scriptures not teach the immutability of God? Indeed they do. They do not, however, teach an abstract immutability in an abstract context. They do not ask whether God is mutable if he blesses Israel today and hides his face from her in judgment tomorrow. The Scriptures do not ask if God is changeable if he threatens Nineveh with destruction for thirty days and then repents and does not destroy it. Biblical thought is too profoundly focused on the realities of God's salvation and judgment to raise theoretical questions about whether God would be a changeable, mutable God if he could turn from his fierce anger and cause his face to shine once more. Instead, when Israel's life is threatened and the destroying winds of judgment blow on her, Israel cries to the Lord to have pity on her and deliver her from his anger.

The trouble with an abstract doctrine of divine immutability is that it is at best religiously useless and at worst destructive of true religion. Such immutability surely has no place, for example, in prayer or worship. The immutable God of decretal theology and the singular decree, a God without pathos, a God who cannot be touched either by the infirmities, or the anguish, or, for that matter, the wickedness of the world, is a far cry from the biblical God who as a father loves his children, gives his own Son for the redemption of the world, hates iniquity, and can send his judgment on the sin and evil of the world. The God of the Bible is a living and personal God, a God who is more than logic, a God who freely reacts to the world in both grace and judgment, a God who is deeply involved in man's history, as his election of Israel and his covenant-making with her richly demonstrate.

It is exactly in the religious arena of divine grace that the Bible speaks of the immutability of God. God's immutability is not located somewhere outside the historical context, which must then somehow be related to an abstractly conceived doctrine of God and his decree. Decretal theology demonstrates the impossibility of relating an abstract doctrine of divine immutability or of a divine decree to religious realities. The best it can do is assert that the world cannot touch God and that God cannot be and is not free to be touched by the world. Such a concept of immutability undermines the realities of man's sin, God's wrath, and God's freedom. Hoeksema not only lost "man as a sinner" as the object of the divine love, he also lost a place in his theology, as do all decretal theologians, for the reality and the historical character of God's wrath. An abstract doctrine of divine immutability (whether of God or of his decree or of both) inevitably ends up losing such historical realities as sin, divine wrath, judgment on and hatred of sin, and must read these back into the nature of God.

The doctrine of immutability that the Bible presents, within the context of man's sin and God's grace and judgment, is burdened with none of these serious difficulties. God is free to bless Israel today and punish her tomorrow, to threaten Nineveh today and withdraw the threat tomorrow.[7] And it is

---

[7] In biblical thought God can turn away his wrath precisely because "I am God and not man . . . the Holy One in the midst of thee" (Hos. 11:9). This kind of divine turning aside of wrath (repentance, change) may not have its meaning

precisely this recognition of divine freedom that informs Israel's cries for deliverance and prayers for a new day of mercy.

The Bible discusses God's immutability within the religious context of man's sin and God's judgment and grace, and in full recognition of the freedom of God. In biblical thought God is always free to repent of the evil that he said he would do to Nineveh and not do it. His judgments in history on Israel, on the church, on the world are always conditional. Judgments, therefore, can be real divine threats though they do not materialize.[8] It is only within the authentic religious context that one can understand God's repentance, that is, within that context of sin and grace in which God possesses the freedom to respond in grace to Nineveh's repentance and not bring about the evil he threatened. For every man's cry of repentance and call for mercy presupposes this freedom of God to forgive and deliver from the judgment of the law.

Where God is clearly immutable is in the area of grace. Once God makes covenant promise, he cannot recall it. To it he has attached his oath. Once God makes himself the husband of Israel and Israel his wife, he cannot abandon her.[9] Though Israel commits spiritual adultery with other gods, Yahweh does not and cannot divorce Israel. Though an Israelite husband was freed from his wife through her adultery, God was not free to divorce an adulterous Israel. Paul puts it plainly. God has not cast off Israel, his people, "for the gifts and the call of God are irrevocable" (Rom. 11:29).

"What if some were unfaithful? Does their faithlessness nullify the faithfulness of God? By no means!" (Rom. 3:3, 4). God's faithfulness is not in the least degree changed or mitigated by Israel's unbelief. Hence the recurring emphasis in the Old Testament on the faithfulness of God. The psalm-

drained off through the filter of an alleged anthropomorphism because its possibility lies in the expressed fact that God is "God and not man."

[8] There are, therefore, real possibilities that are never actualized. This decretal theologians disallow. They contend that there are no *real* possibilities that are not actualized. All authentic possibilities become actualized. They not only deny that what is actualized might not have been, but also affirm that whatever truly "might have been" will surely happen.

[9] This is not an abstract "cannot" but one that resides in God's free decision to remain the husband of Israel in spite of her desire for other gods.

ist can say over and over again that "his steadfast love endures forever" (Ps. 136). Indeed it is precisely this unfailing and unchanging faithfulness of God that constitutes Paul's profound struggle with the fact of Israel's unbelief in Romans 9-11.

The answer to Paul's struggle is not the simple one that some Israelites were reprobates. Were that the case, three of the most profound chapters in the New Testament would not have been necessary. Indeed, it is the emphasis on God's unchanging faithfulness that accounts for the acknowledged universalist strain in biblical thought. In Romans 11:32 Paul, thinking of Jews and Gentiles, declares that "God has consigned all men to disobedience, that he may have mercy on all." Apparently this "all" does not refer to Jews and Gentiles as two groups, for then it would have been more natural to speak of "both" rather than "all." And the election of Israel as a nation is said to be the promise that through Israel all nations would be blessed. This does not indeed mean that all men will be saved. It is only to point out the biblical emphasis on the immutability of God's total and unchangeable commitment to be gracious. God cannot divorce Israel and cease to be her husband, not indeed because of anything in Israel, but because of the immutability of his promise and election. God is immutable in his grace, and mutable in his judgment.

This is the kind of divine immutability the Bible speaks of. This kind of immutability is perceived within the tensions and possibilities that obtain within the context of man's sin and God's free grace. This immutability of a gracious God creates no problem for Arminian theology, for which salvation and damnation ultimately depend on human decision anyway. But it does create tensions for Reformed theology, for it posits a God who is immutable in his grace and mutable in his judgments. These are the tensions between Arminianism on the one hand and universalism on the other. Although they are theological tensions arising out of human reflection on God's unchanging faithfulness, they are not abstract, nonreligious problems. Paul grappled with this problem in Romans 9-11, theologically and religiously, but not abstractly. For the sake of an abstract problem he would not have been willing to be accursed of Christ (Rom. 9:1-3). It was out of a deep religious anguish that he struggled theologically and also asserted that he was willing to be accursed for the sake of his brother according to the flesh, that is, the unbelieving Jew.

The usual prooftext quoted by decretal theologians for their version of God's immutability is "I the Lord do not change; therefore you, O sons of Jacob, are not consumed" (Mal. 3:6). An appeal is made to the first half of this statement, but the last half is ignored. This text does not prove that God does not change because nothing touches or alters him. On the contrary, it teaches that the sons of Jacob, in spite of all their sins, are not destroyed because God is immutable in the purpose of his grace. This text is a religious affirmation that God in his gracious purposes is forever immutable. This kind of immutability creates problems for abstract theology, but is the only sure hope of the religious man.

When God's immutability is protected by an impersonal, uninvolved understanding of God's relationship to the world, everything Christian is surrendered. It would seem better to define God's "mutability," that is, his repentance as it related to Nineveh and his change from favor to anger against Israel, in terms of what Isaiah calls his "strange" work (Isa. 28:11). God's anger with and judgment on the sinner are regarded as strange in reference to the fact that he is a God of love. Thus God's hatred is not regarded as one of his attributes, since hatred is the opposite of love and thus sinful. God's hatred is not sinful hate, but the form (and reality) of his burning love, which endures in spite of man's sin and unbelief. This love haunts and follows the sinner even into hell, and thus itself— in relation to the sinner—constitutes hell. God then remains the same, but in conjunction with the persistent sinner his abiding, steadfast love for the sinner causes the sinner to be offended.

In biblical thought the concept of offense is real and significant (though little is done with it in most theological thought). Significantly, it is used in the passive. The sinner takes offense, for example, at the cross. The cross in itself is not offensive, but elicits offense in the sinner. Hence Jesus could say to John the Baptist, "Blessed is he who takes no offense at me" (Luke 7:23). Just as the offense arises *out of the sinner* when Jesus comes into relationship with him, so the God who is unchangeably the God of love and grace when related to the persistent sinner is experienced by the sinner as divine anger, judgment, and rejection. This is an extremely difficult subject, but the area in which an understanding of it should be sought is the area of a profound personal relationship between God and man.

From this perspective—that the God who abidingly loves the world in Jesus Christ determined in his freedom forever to be the God of grace—we must understand the immutability of God. From this perspective we can understand Paul's rhetorical question: "What if some were unfaithful? Does their faithlessness nullify the faithfulness of God?" From this perspective we can group his assertion that all men could be liars, yet the faithfulness of God would abide and remain. From this perspective we can understand his claim that the gifts and calling of God are irrevocable. And this perspective is based on a profoundly *personal* relationship of God to the world and men.

CHAPTER VI

The Election of Israel

The first case of election in the Bible is God's election of the nation of Israel. The Old Testament is the historical record of this divinely chosen people. Though it has rarely been done,[1] serious attention must be given to this first form in which election confronts us. In the first place, the election of this nation and the existence of this nation coincide. Second, Augustine's famous remark—that the New Testament is concealed in the Old Testament and the Old Testament is revealed in the New Testament—is as true about election as it is about any other biblical truth, unless decretal theology is correct in regarding election as a mere instance of an all-encompassing predestination.

A consideration of Israel's election throws helpful light on the biblical teaching about election. This light from the Old Testament has largely been ignored by all those ecclesiastical traditions which have formed a doctrine of individual election, for all of them try to define the election of individuals by a direct reference to an eternal divine decision. Such a direct reference to eternity tends to produce a highly individualistic, ahistorical conception of election. In the Old Testament Israel's election and her covenant status go hand in

[1] In the preface to his *Biblical Doctrine of Election* (1950), H. H. Rowley explains his omission of a bibliography on the ground that so little has been written recently on election. Rowley's discussion concerns the election of Israel, and of individuals within it, chiefly in terms of a conditional election to service rather than to salvation.

99

hand. In electing Israel, God makes covenant with her. As any student of Reformed theology knows, Reformed theology has had acute difficulties in relating the truth of the covenant with individual election.

By approaching election in the first form in which it was historically actualized, we can protect ourselves against an individualistic distortion of election and a premature flight into the realms of eternity. For if the meaning of Christ's election lies concealed in the election of Israel and the meaning of Israel's election is revealed in Christ's election, the election of no individual can be adequately understood in isolation from this context.

Turning to the Old Testament, we confront the first historical revelation of election in God's choosing Abram and calling him from Ur of the Chaldees. Abram, of course, is an individual, but his election is not illustrative of a merely individualistic election. In choosing Abram, God does not choose a single individual; his election includes the election of his seed. There is no election of Abram the individual apart from his seed, and no election of his seed apart from Abram. The object of God's election is the nation that flows from Abram and of which he is a part.

If we look closely at this object of God's election—and not at something our religious minds or sentiment may conjure up—we discover that the object of this election is, apart from this election, *nothing*. Who is this man who with his seed is chosen by God? He is a man to whom God promises a son. Yet God tarries in granting the son until this man's potentiality for having a son is lost in the passage of years. He becomes an old man, physically (as Paul says) "as good as dead" (Rom. 4:19). When he heard the divine promise that he would have a son, he "fell on his face and laughed, and said to himself, 'Shall a child be born to a man who is a hundred years old? Shall Sarah, who is ninety years old, bear a child?' " (Gen. 17:17). An impotent old man with a barren wife—this is the object, the Israel of God's election. Describing this situation, Paul said of Abraham that "in hope he believed against hope."

In a real sense the object of God's election does not exist. For the object of God's election is not an impotent, childless

old man. The object is not Abram; the object is Abraham, a
man with a son, a father of a great nation. But this does not exist. God's election must produce what it elects. And it does.
Isaac is a son of miracle. Abram and Sarai laughed at the impossibility, but out of the impossibility God creates the possibility
and the actuality, calling "into existence the things that do
not exist" (Rom. 4:17). To indicate the new reality Abram
and Sarai are given the new names of Abraham and Sarah.
And as a poignant reminder through the years, the son who
emerges out of impotency and impossibility must by divine
command (Gen. 17:19) be called Isaac, which means "to
laugh."

On the one hand, election appears as a creation out of
nothing; God calls into existence the things that do not exist.
On the other hand, election appears as the creation of something out of its *opposite,* a divine act that gives life to the
dead (Rom. 4:17), that creates possibility out of impossibility, that turns Sarai's laugh of cynicism and doubt into
Sarah's laugh of joy (Gen. 21:6). Indeed, Paul compares this
elective action of God with his act that "raised from the dead
Jesus our Lord" (Rom. 4.24). But whether God's elective act
is regarded as an act of creation out of nothing, or an act of
creation out of something opposite, election appears in any
case as a creative act, an act that creates what it elects.

On the basis of the Old Testament narrative concerning
Abraham and the birth of his son, and Paul's New Testament
interpretation of this Old Testament narrative, it must be said
that the nation of Israel is not viewed as one extant nation
among many, which is then selectively chosen by God as his
elect people. Rather, Israel as the object of God's election
not only does not exist but even has no possibility of existence apart from God's elective and creative action. The
nation that is the seed of Abraham owes its existence to this
mysterious and inexplicable act of God.

This same emphasis on the truth that God creates what he
elects appears from a consideration of the divine promise that
Abraham will be the father of *many* nations. A man who has
many sons can indeed be the father of many nations, but not
the father of one son. But the promise to Abraham that he
will be the father of many nations is realized through one

son. For "through Isaac shall your descendants be named"
(Gen. 21:12). Again it appears that what God elected
Abraham to be, God must himself provide; and the object of
God's election again becomes the product of his own creative
action. The truth of this is further exemplified in the suc-
ceeding generation. Isaac had two sons, Jacob and Esau, but
one of these is rejected by God as a medium through which
the "many nations" shall emerge. In his dealing with both
Abraham and his son Isaac, God demonstrates that the object
of his election will not be Abraham's or Isaac's creation but
his own creation.

The correlation of Israel's election and her creation as it
appears in the history of Abraham, Sarah, and Isaac is explicated not only by the New Testament commentary on this
history, but also in the Book of Isaiah. Some of the richest,
most beautiful passages of Scripture are found in Isaiah
40-66. But ministers of the gospel are more apt to read these
passages than they are to preach on them. The great theme of
these chapters is comfort. "Comfort, comfort my people,
says your God" (Isa. 40:1). Why does the church constantly
resort to these texts for comfort? Why do ministers of the
gospel constantly go to them for consolation in the face of
their own needs and their congregations' needs, yet infre-
quently use them as texts for sermons? Perhaps it is because
these passages make election and creation correlatives, and
thereby appeal to the heart but stagger and confound the
mind.

What is the basis of the comfort that forms the grand
theme of the final chapters of Isaiah? Is it not that the
election and the creation of Israel are correlatives, that the
one is the demonstration of the truth and fact of the other?
According to these chapters, Israel—even in an exile that
seems to belie her special status before God—is to find her
fountain of comfort in the fact that she exists because of her
election, and that in spite of the temporarily wretched form
of her existence she will never be forsaken by the God who
chooses her. This correlation of Israel's election and existence
may indeed surpass our comprehension, but this truth is
presented to an exiled people for consolation and comfort.
Israel must take comfort in her uncomfortable situation

because she knows that she was created by God and exists because of her election. God who is the creator of the ends of the earth is Israel's creator. He who formed her in the womb called her and created her by *naming* her. The God who chose Israel maintains his covenant with her. By his power and decision Israel, though barren, will be the fruitful mother of children. Through this all, the theme is that of the Almighty God, who will fulfil his counsel, none being able to stay his hand, the God who received counsel and direction from no one—the theme Paul takes up at the close of Romans 11.

We shall quote here only those texts that deal most explicitly with this correlation between Israel's creation and her election. These passages constantly recall the dealings of God with Abraham and form an expansive commentary on these dealings:

> But now thus says the Lord, he who created you, O Jacob, he who formed you, O Israel: "Fear not, for I have redeemed you; I have called you by name, you are mine" (Isa. 43:1).
>
> "I will say to the north, Give up, and to the south, Do not withhold; bring my sons from afar and my daughters from the end of the earth, every one who is called by my name, whom I created for my glory, whom I formed and made" (Isa. 43:6, 7).
>
> "I am Lord, your Holy One, the Creator of Israel" (Isa. 43:15).
>
> "I give water in the wilderness, rivers in the desert, to give drink to my chosen people, the people whom I formed for myself" (Isa. 43:20, 21).
>
> "But now hear, O Jacob my servant, Israel whom I have chosen! Thus says the Lord who made you, who formed you from the womb and will help you: Fear not, O Jacob my servant, Jeshurun whom I have chosen" (Isa. 44:1, 2).
>
> "The Lord called me from the womb, from the body of my mother he named my name" (Isa. 49:1).
>
> "Kings shall see and arise; princes, and they shall prostrate themselves; because of the Lord, who is faithful, the Holy One of Israel, who has chosen you" (Isa. 49:7).

Even from these few passages it is clear that in biblical thought the nation of Israel is God's creation and Israel *as such* is the object of his election. Her election to be God's covenant people is the ground and meaning of her creation.

Israel's election and her creation are two intermingling and interpenetrating aspects of the one divine determination and decision that she is to be God's people.

The definition of individual election as "the unchangeable purpose of God, whereby, before the foundation of the world, He has . . . chosen from the whole human race . . . a certain number of persons" (Canons of Dort, I, 7), whatever its merit as a description of individual election, does not cover the election of the nation of Israel. The whole thrust of the story of God's establishment of his covenant with Abraham and his seed, together with the material we have cited from Isaiah, speaks of election on a quite different level than that of a selection out of a mass humanity.

It would appear, then, that election, as we first encounter it in the Old Testament, is national, not merely individual. This election indeed includes the individual, but only within the larger scope of the nation. God calls and elects, establishes his covenant with, and makes his futuristic promises with, Abraham *and his seed.*

Divine election in its basic Old Testament form is collective, corporate, national. It encompasses a community of which the individual Israelite is an integral part. In the New Testament, this form of election is not atomized and undone but fulfilled. Furthermore, the historical account of Genesis, which is theologically interpreted in Isaiah, makes it apparent that the object of God's election, as disclosed in the Old Testament, is no concrete, historical object that exists independently of God's election. God's elective action is not a selection of one historical reality out of many historical realities. On the contrary, in his elective action, God creates what he elects.

God can, of course, only *reveal* his grace and gracious election to existent man. But if actual existent men in history are to understand the true nature of God's gracious election, they must learn that their very existence is the result of God's gracious election. It is God's election that constitutes Israel as a nation. Her very existence is grounded in God's decision to be her God and to bear everlastingly the name: "The God of your fathers, the God of Abraham, the God of Isaac, and the God of Jacob . . . this is my name for ever, and thus I am to be remembered throughout all generations" (Exod. 3:15). God chooses to bear the name of Abraham, Isaac, and Jacob forever and to be ever known and remembered by that name. The future of God is forever tied to this people that he has chosen and created for himself. Thus Israel's reality and future and God's own future and name are indissolubly bound together.

The idea that Israel owes her very existence to God's election and creative action is further supported by the Old Testament teaching that God is the Father of Israel and Israel is God's son. This is clear from Psalm 2. Psalm 2 is a messianic Psalm, but everything it prophetically declares about Christ had earlier been said by God about Israel: the promise of victory over enemies, the promise of the nations as inheritance, the promise that those who blessed (kissed) her would be blessed and those who cursed her would be cursed. The writer of Psalm 2 described the Messiah in terms that were in the first instance applicable to Israel as a nation. And the central affirmation in this Psalm is "You are my Son, today I have begotten you" (vs. 7). This teaching is simply an anticipation of what Isaiah declared when he asserted that God created Israel as a nation and formed her in the womb. Israel, like the Christ, has no father but God, and, like the Christ, is God's peculiar and unique son.

This same truth is given personal individual expression in Psalm 139. The writer of Psalm 139 declares that God knows him and that there is no escape from this divine knowing in heaven, Sheol, or the uttermost parts of the earth. Why?

> For thou didst form my inward parts, thou didst knit me together in my mother's womb. I praise thee, for thou art fearful and wonderful. Wonderful are thy works! Thou knowest me right well. . . . Thy eyes beheld my unformed substance; in thy book were written, every one of them, the days that were formed for me, when as yet there was none of them (vv. 13-16).

Israel in her corporate national form and her individual personal form, and even the days that were formed for her time and history, "when as yet there was none of them," was known, and called, and chosen by God. The nation no less than the individual Israelite was, in the words of Psalm 139, "made in secret, intricately wrought in the depths of the earth" (vs. 15).

If this is a substantially correct report of the election of Israel as we see it in the Old Testament, we may sum up as follows. The election of Israel is the election of a nation rather than an election of individuals. Israel's election and creation are inseparable. God does not elect what is (Abram, impotent and childless) but what is not (Abraham the father of a great nation, even many nations), and thus creates what he elects. Israel is not a nation fathered by someone other than God and later adopted by God as a stepson; it is rather a nation fathered, begotten, elected, and created by God himself. Israel's existence is grounded in God's election. And all this is reflected in the ground and nature of the covenant.

*   *   *

This sketch of the structure of the Old Testament view of Israel's election shows it to be much too rich and complex to be contained within the traditional classical view of individual election. It also obviously differs from a view of election as a divine selection out of a fallen human race. Such a difference, however, is something that even the traditional Reformed theology of election tolerates. Supralapsarianism is regarded as tolerable within the modern understanding of Reformed orthodoxy; and one of the distinctive features of the supralapsarian view is that the initial act of divine election and reprobation has no objects and that the creation of the objects of such elective and rejective divine action logically follows such elective action. Furthermore, if what we have said is substantially faithful to the notion of election as it appears in the Old Testament, we may expect significant elements of this view to reappear in the form in which election confronts us in the New Testament.

We are not suggesting that there is no elective selection within the national election of Israel. The Old Testament, in fact, presents us with such an elective movement *within* the national election of Israel, which progressively narrows and concentrates on representative individuals, and finally on a single individual who is uniquely *the* seed of Abraham and

THE ELECTION OF ISRAEL

the Son of David, Jesus of Nazareth, whom God made to be both Lord and Christ. The movement of God's elective and creative action may be illustrated by concentric circles that rise like a cone from a wide base until they reach their peak where the whole is concentrated in a single point. From the broad base of Abraham and his seed God's elective action moves toward him who is the true Israel of God; from the many prophets of God to the Chief Prophet, himself the Word of God; from the many Old Testament priests to the only High Priest; from many kings to the true Son of David who will rule forever over a kingdom that has no end; from Abraham's seed which numbered as the stars of the heavens and the sands on the seashore to Abraham's seed which, says Paul, is Christ and is not many seeds but one (Gal. 3:16). God's elective and creative action moves from a nation who is the suffering servant of God, the light of the Gentiles, created by God as a covenant for the peoples and projected as the hope of the ends of the earth, to him who came in the form of a servant, whose blood is the blood of the new covenant, and who is the glory of Israel and the Light of the world.

Such an elective-creative movement of God in Israel's history carries with it a displacement of Israel's prophets, priests, and kings, her synagogues and temple, her laws and covenant until there is room for one only: Jesus Christ. Every datum of Old Testament Israel is displaced, but in such a way that it finds its fulfilment through its displacement. Everything in Israel's history has its history, for everything moves toward its eschatological goal, its fulfilment in that fulness of time when Christ emerges out of Israel's election and creation as the ultimate purpose and fulfilment of them.

This process of narrowing does not spell the rejection of all those excluded from the priority of that elective and creative action of God which makes Jesus the Christ, God's chosen. If that were so, Jesus' election would be the annulment rather than the fulfilment of Israel's creation and election. God's election of Jesus does fulfil the purpose of Israel's election—to be a blessing to Israel and, through Israel, to all nations. God's election of Israel achieved its purpose only in Jesus Christ, for only in him did Israel become a blessing to all the families of the earth. The unique and peculiar election of Jesus Christ itself excluded no man or family or tribe or nation in the world. It only excluded that sinful pride by which any man or family or tribe or nation would make itself *the* Elect of God, *the* man (or family, tribe, or nation) of destiny, *the* one through which God would deal with all other men.

A doctrine of individual election that appeals to Old Testament history for proof of individual election but fails to see this history as a movement converging on Jesus of Nazareth has not sensed the meaning of the Old Testament's doctrine of election.

This does not mean that every Israelite displaced by Jesus Christ is a saved individual. But from the historical actualization of the election of Christ one may not infer the rejection of the nation of Israel. For if Israel is rejected, how could Christ be the *fulfilment* of her election, covenant, law, prophets, priests, and kings, and the embodiment of her glory? Christ emerges in New Testament thought as *the* seed of Abraham, *the* son of David, and as the one who is, as the personification of Israel's election, *the* elect of God.

We must save for a later chapter the question whether these distinctive ingredients of Israel's election—its nonindividualistic form and the correlation between it and Israel's creation—appear in the New Testament portrayal of the election of Jesus Christ. Suffice it here to point out first that Jesus Christ emerges on the pages of the New Testament as the unique and only begotten Son of God who nonetheless has many brethren (Rom. 8:29); as one who can say "Here am I, and the children God has given me" (Heb. 2:13); as one crucified alone though in his death all have died (II Cor. 5:14); as one who arose alone, yet in his resurrection the "many" also arise; as one who alone ascended into heaven, yet in his ascension we are seated with Christ in the heavenly places and now have our citizenship in heaven. Indeed, Christ appears in the New Testament as the firstborn of every creature, the firstfruits of them that slept, the one in whom all Christians have been created and elected, the one in whom the Christian's life is hidden, the one to whom belong all kingdom, power, and glory, yet as one who shares all three with the church, and publicly demonstrates and reveals them in the church that is called to recapitulate his life, death, triumph, service, and mission as he himself recapitulated the calling, service, and history of Israel. The New Testament, in short, knows nothing of a Christ who is the elect of God apart from Israel, nor anything of a Christ who is God's elect apart from a church that shares in all that he is and will be.

Is the correlation of Israel's election and creation reflected in the New Testament in Jesus Christ? Again the answer must be yes. Jesus Christ is indeed the seed of Abraham, yet of the Abraham who is past age and has no seed. Jesus Christ is also the "Son of David." Jesus is born of Mary, but of Mary the virgin, who can only wonder in her perplexity how such things can be. Joseph is a descendant of David through the line of Solomon, the royal strand that has the right of the crown, yet Joseph is by clear New Testament teaching excluded from any part in fathering Jesus. Furthermore, Christ is born, not by the will of man, nor by the will or power of the nation of Israel. He is born of Israel at a time when she is spiritually and politically bankrupt, as the genealogy in the very opening chapter of the New Testament indicates.

When the fulness of time comes, a time historically ripe for the disclosure of God's revelation of the meaning of his elective and creative action, Jesus is born. As Isaac was born when there was no potentiality in Abraham for bringing forth the son necessary for his seed to be called, the son through whom alone he could be a father of many nations and a blessing to all the nations of the earth, so the Christ is born to the throne of David and called by God to be a blessing to all the nations of the earth at a time when Israel is occupied country, governed by a pagan power, when her prophetic voice had been silent for three centuries, when the descendant of her royal family is wielding a hammer instead of a scepter. When Abraham is as good as dead, God calls life from the dead and himself creates Isaac, thereby creating what he elects. When Israel is spiritually and politically bankrupt, without kingdom, power, or glory, God himself provides the kingdom, power and glory and through his Spirit begets Jesus Christ, thereby creating the object that is *par excellence* his choice and delight, the true Representative of Israel, God's Elect.

It is from this perspective that we must view the origin of both the Christian man and the Christian church. The Christian's origin is in that creative, regenerative act of the Spirit of God which Reformed theology describes as an occurrence below the level of the individual's consciousness and thus hidden from his eyes, an event inaccessible to man's memory or investigation. It is precisely the followers of those theological traditions which assert that the dead sinner's transition to a new life in Christ is the result of his decision for Christ who are always prone to make God's election contingent on human decision. If the sinner can re-create himself into a believer, if he can bring life out of death, if he can first choose God so that God then chooses him and utters the divine Amen, then the sinner, without divine intervention, can effect both his own election and his own creation as a Christian. But if creation and election belong to God alone, then God does both and thus creates what he elects.

It is also from this perspective that we must view the origin and reality of the church. The church is a reality in history—this is the church's confession in its early apostolic creed. *I believe a holy, Catholic church.* The church confesses its faith, not in itself, but in the fact of its existence. The reality of the church—and the reality of Christian existence—is an object of faith and remains, for all its historical actuality, an object of faith. For the existence of the church, as the existence of its individual members, has its ground in that mystery of Isaac's birth, in the mystery of Israel's divine creation and election; and both have their ultimate ground in the shadow that falls over God's act as it fell over Mary when the Almighty came upon her and created him whom he chose above all others.

Given this mysterious origin and character of the church, it is not surprising that after twenty centuries the church is still baffled, confused, and unable to provide a definite doctrine of itself. Is the reason for the paucity of understanding of the church within the church the fact that the divine action that accounts for the existence of the church is an elective and creative action, thus rendering the ground of the church something that evades the grasp of the church?

Christian theologians are unlikely to deny the corporate character of Israel's election, for its reality on the biblical page is too stark to deny. But it has been ignored. And no theological tradition with a doctrine of election seems troubled that its doctrine of election does not contain—and cannot absorb without modification—the corporate, national election of Israel.

Serious theological concern with Israel as a nation has been largely the province of premillennial thinkers. Since this theology is in fact usually Arminian, and Arminianism is essentially individualistic, their concern does not cover the peculiar character of Israel's election. Mainstream theological traditions, particularly the Reformed, have dissolved the corporate feature of Israel's election in their doctrine of individual election. What is seen in Israel's peculiar election are individual elect Jews. Even the extraordinary election of Jesus is taken to be largely similar to any man's election. And God's elective-creative act, moving through Abraham and his seed down through the years until Christ, is almost wholly ignored. Berkhof, for example, in his *Systematic Theology* gives eight lines to discussing Christ's predestination. In his discussion of the biblical view of election, Christ's election is not even mentioned. And under the same heading the election of Israel is given less than two lines.

Reformed theology has also dissolved Israel's corporate election by regarding it as a merely historical, passing phenomenon. Once upon a time the Jewish nation was God's chosen people. But the Jews as a nation rejected and crucified Jesus of Nazareth, and again as a nation rejected Christ as he came to them in the proclamation of the gospel. Admittedly there are individual elect Jews now and then who believe in Christ and are saved, but the nation as a nation is lost. In judgment God has turned from the Jewish nation to the Gentiles. Most Reformed theologians—and Reformed Christians generally—do not believe that the Jews as a nation have a religious future. Thus Berkhof defines Israel's election merely as an election "for special privileges and for special service." The definition does not include the idea of salvation, and indeed most Reformed theologians do not include the idea of salvation in their concept of Israel's election.[2] Elect Israel never had a religious future, not even prior to the crucifixion in the Old Testament times.

There are serious defects in this way of disposing of the corporate election of Israel. First of all, it is the only instance of theological election that is not related to salvation. The election of individuals, of the church, and even of Christ (in a very modified, yet real, sense) is always an election to salvation. Second, if Israel's election is not to salvation, but merely to special privilege and special service, the argument that God has rejected the nation because it rejected the Christ collapses. If God did not elect the nation for salvation, its elective status before God cannot be undone because it rejected salvation. Third, this disposal of the corporate election of the nation of Israel clashes head on with Paul's assertion in Romans 11 about election. Against the background of the discussion of Israel's unbelief in Romans 9 and 10, Romans 11 raises the question: "Has God rejected his people?" and answers it with a ringing "By no means!" Toward the end of the chapter Paul speaks of the nation of Israel, of its partial hardening, of the fact that Israel is an enemy of the gospel, but he declares that this is for the sake (salvation) of the Gentiles. But Israel is not, therefore, God's enemy. On the contrary, "as regards election," the nation is "beloved for the sake of their forefathers." Proof? "For the gifts and the call of God are irrevocable" (Rom. 11:29).

God's election of Israel is not merely to special privilege and special service. Her election is no mere passing historical phenomenon of temporary privilege and service. It is to salvation. "All Israel will be saved" (11:26), and this is certain because the gifts and calling of God are irrevocable. God called a nation, and the election of this nation is not subject to a divine change of mind. Why not? Paul does not urge the immutability of God. He urges rather that Israel's election is not undone because of God's love for their forefathers. God had chosen Abraham and his seed, and the election of God persists both forward from fathers to chil-

2 Nonetheless, there is a consensus among Reformed theologians that election is not merely a summons to service.

dren, and backward from children to fathers. Even the nation's unbelief cannot undo God's election of it. Paul's whole argument contradicts the idea that God's election of the nation of Israel is merely an historical, passing thing, something of special privilege and service but not salvific.

Is Israel's special privilege lost through unbelief? In Romans 3 Paul answers this question, and the answer is the substance of his discussion in Romans 10 and 11. In the first two chapters of Romans Paul had urged that the Jew, although he had the law, was no less than the Gentile under the condemnation of God. He imagines that the Jews may protest and appeal to their special status before God, asking, "What advantage has the Jew?" (Rom 3:1). Paul does not deny their special status before God; in fact, he confirms it. "Much in every way" (vs. 2). The Jew, says Paul, has an advantage because he was given the oracles (revelation) of God, and this advantage is not dissipated by the fact that some Jews did not believe in Christ (vv. 2-4). The faithfulness of God—God's commitment to his gracious election—will not and cannot be undone! The Jews have special gifts and privileges, and the advantage of these remains even when the Jew is under the same condemnation as the Gentile. No sin or unbelief on the part of some, or of the nation as a whole, can undo either this advantage or God's faithfulness. The unrighteousness of men, says Paul, does not annul the righteousness and faithfulness of God; on the contrary, it only makes God's righteousness and faithfulness more obvious.

In Romans 11 we again encounter the idea that God uses man's sin to further the righteousness and faithfulness of his elective purpose. Here Paul reveals the mystery that through Israel's unbelief salvation is opened up to the Gentiles. But even this occurs, he asserts, to provoke the Jews to jealousy, so that they may also be saved and God's election of Israel to salvation may stand. Even the salvation of the Gentiles, according to Paul, occurs for the sake of God's election of the nation of Israel. Gentiles are saved and through this God's election of the nation of Israel is both actualized and demonstrated.

This priority of the national election of corporate Israel over the election of Gentiles is reflected in Paul's definition of the gospel as that in which the righteousness of God is revealed, as "the power of God for salvation . . . to the Jew first and then also to the Greek [the Gentile]" (Rom. 1:16-17). God's corporate election of the nation of Israel, and his immutable and faithful commitment to this election, is no mere temporary, passing thing. Just as it is not undone by Israel's unbelief, so it is not displaced by the election and salvation of the Gentiles. On the contrary, the election and salvation of the Gentiles is a means by which God achieves and demonstrates the purpose of his election of the nation of Israel.

Romans 9-11 does not form a biblical commentary on the truth of individual election. Rather, it is a commentary on the fact and the inviolability of God's election of Israel as a nation. If Paul had meant to demonstrate the truth of individual election and reprobation, these chapters would hardly have been some of the most difficult in the New Testament. In these chapters Paul struggles on the one hand with Israel's unbelief in the light of her election, and on the other hand reveals the mystery that Israel's unbelief results in the salvation of the Gentiles, who are saved in order that the purpose of God's election of Israel may be achieved.

One thing is clear from Romans, especially chapters 9-11: no doctrine of individual election, whether of Jew or Gentile, can claim full biblical sanction unless it takes its shape and definition from and within God's election of the nation of Israel. In other words, the Bible knows nothing of an *isolated, individualistic* doctrine of election;[3] it knows only of a divine election that involves both the father and his seed, one that moves in history "throughout their generations." The Bible knows nothing of an individual election with a direct reference to eternity; it knows only of a divine election that is historical, one that moves and is actualized in the continu-

---

[3] Election, says G. C. Berkouwer, is neither individualistic nor collectivistic. The individual's election is not smothered by a collectivistic election. Because election is in Christ, the individual is related to Christ the elect cornerstone. Thus, in biblical thought there is no tension between the election of the individual and the election of the church. The nature of election, thus, is not inherently exclusive of others, and to think that it is Berkouwer calls "the great misconception," which turns individual election into proud self-esteem. *Divine Election,* pp. 309f.

ity of father and son, family and nation. As there are no more individuals like Melchizedek, without father and mother, so there is no individual election that is not also a social, corporate election.

We shall discuss this bond between individual and collective, which is constitutive of both the individual and the nation, at greater length in our chapter on the election of the church, where it will also be shown that the very election and salvation of the Gentiles is contingent on the persistent character of God's election of Israel.

CHAPTER VII

The Election of Jesus Christ

No responsible Christian theologian has ever denied the election of Jesus, but throughout church history this has always remained more implicit than explicit. Jesus' election is an unspoken, working assumption that never becomes the center of theological awareness and concern. Christian thought has probed into almost every conceivable aspect of the person and work of Jesus, but his election has rarely, except in the thought of Karl Barth, been the object of special theological investigation.

This oversight is especially strange in election-conscious theological traditions. Concentrating on the election of the individual as a doctrine of special interest, they have developed sophisticated theological constructions of individual election, but their great concern with individual election has never led to an equal concern with the election of Jesus.

There is an historical explanation—if not a theological justification—for this inattentiveness to Jesus' election. The church's first serious concern with the doctrine of election arose at the time of Augustine with its concern over the doctrines of sin and grace. Later, during the Reformation (particularly in Calvin), concern with election arose again within a soteriological concern about sin and grace. Since Jesus did not stand at the center of this concern, he did not fall within the church's concern about election. This narrow interest in the individual's salvation and election accounts, we might add, for the church's equal disinterest in the election

of Israel and of the church. This disinterest cannot be justified theologically, because the election of Israel and the
church can illumine the nature of sin and grace.

Nor was scholasticism—either in its medieval or its Protestant variety—conditioned to have concern for the election of
Jesus. Both were interested in a much wider concept of
predestination as an all-comprehensive decree by which God
determined all things. Election was absorbed into predestination, and predestination was discussed in systematic theology
where God—not man's salvation—is discussed. Their conviction was that election or non-election of individuals cannot
be distinguished from the divine predestination of all things—
the fall of a sparrow or the score of a football game. Within
this theological perspective the election of Jesus was precluded from special consideration. And from this theological
perspective there is, of course, no more reason to preach on
the election of the individual—to say nothing of preaching on
the election of Israel or the church—than there is to preach
on yesterday's fallen sparrow or today's football score.

Calvin in effect rejected this reduction of election by
taking it out of the doctrine of God and placing it in the
doctrine of salvation. He was convinced that election could
not be understood exclusively in terms of God, apart from
man's sin and God's free grace. He understood election condi-
tionally, that is, as God's free response to man's fallen condition. Within this perspective, Calvin spoke of Christ as the
"mirror of election," by which he meant that the whole truth
of God's election is reflected in Jesus Christ. Since we are
elected "in Christ," Calvin urges, we must not look for
knowledge of election in God apart from Jesus Christ. "If we
are elected in him, we cannot find the certainty of our
election in ourselves; and not even in God the Father, if we
look at him apart from the Son."[1]

This insight of Calvin was, however, soon lost. Beza, Calvin's successor, returned election to the doctrine of God;
Reformed scholasticism left it there; and that is where it has
remained. Every typical Reformed—and Lutheran—systemat-

---

[1] *Institutes* III. xxiv. 5. Calvin can be quoted in support of contrary positions,
but this statement—and, more than that, his deliberate break with the traditional
dogmatic location of election—indicates his basic perspective on the doctrine.

ic theology treats election in its opening section, which deals
with the doctrine of God. Scholastic decretal theology developed what we might call "decree-monism," in which the
decree is everything.

But though the church's doctrine of election arose in
contexts (sin and grace, the single decree) not calculated to
generate serious concern with the election of Jesus, it remains
strange that Christian theology has shown so little interest in
the election of Jesus. As we have seen, the issue at the cross
was precisely the election of Jesus, and the cross is admittedly at the center of Christian truth. In song and sermon the
church has fixed its mind on the derision and cruel mockery
hurled upon the suffering Christ, yet it has rarely inquired
into the reason for that mockery. What was central at the
cross one would expect to lie close to the center of Christian
theology.

The neglect of Jesus' election is strange for still another
reason. The election of Jesus is, after all, theological shorthand for the truth that Jesus is the Christ—the central affirmation of the New Testament, the core of the early church's
proclamation, the theme of Peter's Pentecost sermon. For
preaching Jesus as the Christ, the early apostles were arrested
and jailed, and on being beaten and released, did it again.
"Every day in the temple and at home they did not cease
teaching and preaching *Jesus as the Christ*" (Acts 5:42). For
preaching that God had elected him whom his hearers had
rejected, Stephen became the first Christian martyr. It was
the belief that Jesus is the Christ, the chosen of God, that led
Saul to lay waste the church of Jerusalem and to journey to
Damascus to attack the Christians there; and it was the
demonstration that Jesus is the Christ on his way to Damascus that triggered his conversion.

Earlier, the fact that Jesus is the Christ was the sermon
topic of the first sermon Jesus himself preached in his home-
town (Luke 4). In the synagogue, on the Sabbath day, he
read from Isaiah 61. "The Spirit of the Lord is upon me,
because he has anointed me." Jesus applied these words of
Isaiah to himself, as his hearers recognized. At the beginning
of his ministry, in his first sermon in his home town, Jesus

identifies himself as the elect of God, on whom God has put his Spirit.

Jesus is the Christ. This was the issue at the cross. This was the substance of the early church's preaching. This was what the early Christians believed and the unbelievers rejected with animus.

Many churches preach Jesus. How many consciously and explicitly preach Jesus *as the Christ?* Few indeed. But the failure explicitly to preach Jesus as the Christ is a kind of implicit separation of Jesus of Nazareth from the Christ of election. It is a kind of historical discrediting of Jesus' true humanity and historicity. The election of Jesus, by God, to be the Christ, was the central issue in the life and proclamation of the early New Testament church.

*   *   *

There has been a pronounced tendency in the history of the church to preach and think of "Christ" apart from Jesus of Nazareth, and particularly apart from the Old Testament out of which he emerged. Where this tendency prevails one would hardly expect that Jesus' election would be seen as rooted deep in the Old Testament and contained in, and a fulfilment and actualization of, Israel's election. In effect, the wide unconcern in Christian theology about Israel's election severs Jesus from his historical roots. Men speak of Christ—particularly Christians—and do not really think of him as a Jew. Some evangelicals think of the incarnation as a brand new creation, not as an assumption of our fallen human nature. Some extremely sectarian Christians are at great pains to try to show that Christ was no Jew but rather a universal man. But separating Christ's election from Jesus of Nazareth tears asunder what belongs together. "Jesus Christ" is really a sentence: Jesus is the Christ; that Jew who was *the* seed of Abraham, *the* son of David, is *the* Elect of God. Hence what the early church believed and preached was neither "Jesus" nor "Christ," but the Jesus whom men crucified and God chose, and by that choice made him to be the Christ.

Recent denials of the deity of Christ have tended to obscure this. When Christ's deity was denied by some, others

rushed to affirm it, and thus the question of deity was placed
at the center of our consciousness about Jesus. This issue was
not at center stage in the New Testament. The New Testament contains clear affirmations of Christ's deity and instances in which Jesus was charged with blasphemy, but the
great issue between Jesus and his contemporaries was more
the question of whether he was elected by God than whether
he was God. His fellow Jews saw Jesus' election as a contradiction of their own election, and the depth of their reaction
against his claim derived from the depth of their conviction
of their own election. When the two clashed the Jews were
deeply offended, and they could not, as did the Greeks and
Romans, simply regard it as foolishness and forget about it.
They saw what was at stake. One had to go.

Jesus' claim to be Son of God did not in itself arouse
Jewish antipathy. After all, they regarded themselves as sons
of God. For the same reason this designation did not in itself
imply a claim of deity for them. But it was the priority and
uniqueness that Jesus claimed for his sonship, election, authority, and word over theirs, and the difference that constituted his priority, that caused the Jews to be offended in the
depths of their religious being. Though they did not understand the true nature of this priority, they did recognize that
Jesus claimed it. Though they did not properly understand
the nature of their own special status before God, they did
recognize the fact of it.

The Jews misunderstood *both*. If Jesus was what he
claimed to be, then the Jewish nation was not what it
thought itself to be. Thus Jesus was a threat to the nation,
and they reasoned that one of the two had to be destroyed.
That is why the mockery at the cross did not turn especially
on whether Jesus was God, but on whether he was the Christ,
the chosen of God.

The term Son of Man, with all its New Testament eschatological meaning, as claimed by Jesus, appears in fact to have
been just as unacceptable to his contemporaries as the term
Son of God. Both designations seem to have meant much the
same thing to the Jew. Jesus projected himself as having a
special status with God, a status that made him their chief
and final prophet, their chief and eternal high priest, their

one and only Lord, the fulfilment of their law, the embodiment of their temple, the substance of their covenant, and indeed the fulfilment and true meaning of their election.

* * *

The most distinctive thing that can be said about Israel is that she is the nation chosen by God. This can be said of no other nation ancient or modern. God chose the Jewish people as an agent of his redemptive purpose in human history. God has "not dealt thus with any other nation" (Ps. 147:20). God's election always has an historical and eschatological character. Similarly, it is always a call to service, a call to serve God's salvific purpose. The election of Israel, therefore, included a special privilege, the privilege of being called to be co-laborers with God in the realization of his elective purpose. The special service and privilege required special gifts to qualify it for the service required. Obviously, no nation can take this honor on itself (cf. Heb. 5:4) or qualify itself for this task.

But the nation of Israel was not elected merely to render this service to others. It was called itself to share in the redemptive purpose it served. Israel's election in biblical thought is a summons to serve and to share in that for which she is elected. This election is shared by no other ancient or modern nation. Lorraine Boettner loses sight of the unique character of Israel's election when he suggests that some modern nations are also elect nations.[2] Theologically speaking, there is only one step between a Germany that regards itself as divinely elected and a Hitler.[3] No nation, other than Israel, in all the long reaches of history is or ever will be an elect nation. To surrender this uniqueness and exclusiveness of Israel is to forfeit the uniqueness and exclusiveness of the election of Jesus Christ. The quality of Jesus' election to be the Christ is contingent on the history and reality of Israel, because God in his freedom decided to achieve the reality of

[2] *The Reformed Doctrine of Predestination*, p. 88.

[3] Charles Lutz, *So I Have a Choice?* Though arguing an Arminian position, Lutz has some significant things to say about current "chosen nation mentalities" and "national manifest destiny," subjects that cry for fuller exploration.

Jesus as the Christ through the election of Israel, that is, through the election of Abraham and his seed. Abraham and his seed are indispensable to Jesus' election as the Christ only because God in his freedom chose to actualize his election through the nation of the Jews. God willed that his Elect be a Jew, a son of Abraham, one who emerges from that divine elective and creative activity that first gave reality to Israel. Jesus as the Christ is the product of Israel, even as Israel was the product of God. The reality of his election, therefore, is historically grounded in the election of the nation of Israel. It is real only if Israel's election is real.

The basic question here is: How did Jesus as the Christ become an historical reality? And the biblical answer is, through God's election and creation of Israel and his continuing elective and creative action within Israel's history from which the reality of Jesus as the Christ emerged. Or, to put it simply, "salvation is from the Jews" (John 4:22) or there is none at all; Christ is from the Jews, or there is no Christ. This does not mean that God could not work out his redemption of man without human cooperation and compliance. How could it mean that if Israel's reality is the product of God's elective and creative action? There is an unbreakable unity and continuity between Israel and Christ, between Israel's election and Jesus' election. The fact that the reality of the latter depends on the former only indicates the path that God *chose* to actualize his elective and creative production of Jesus as the Christ.

Thus Jesus' election is both dependent on Israel's election and a fulfilment of it. The goal toward which Israel's election and its required special service was directed was achieved and fulfilled in Jesus Christ, and history in the Old Testament sense came to an end. The eschatological end of Israel's election was reached in the reality of Jesus as the Christ; after the end is reached all things become new. Even the Old Testament itself exists in the form of the New Testament. But the New Testament cannot dispense with the Old, nor with the election of Israel.

The depth of this becomes apparent if we recognize that the indispensability of the Old for the New and of Israel's election for that of Jesus Christ are not mere concessions to our knowledge. The point is not that we could not *under-stand* the New without the Old, Jesus' election apart from Israel's, as though Old Testament teaching about Israel's election were some sort of primer for our feeble understanding. The point is that we can only understand the New in the light of the Old because the Old and New are of *one piece*. When we fully understand this in the world to come, we will need neither the Old nor the New Testament Scriptures. For then we shall see Christ face to face and know him as one whose election is inextricably bound up with the election of Israel in its very role as the fulfilment of Israel's election. We shall then see clearly that Israel's election is an essential ingredient of Jesus' election, and that we could not have the one without the other.

So far as the church's understanding of Jesus' election is concerned, it does indeed need the Old Testament. And when the church no longer needs the Old Testament for its knowledge, it can also dispense with the New Testament. But the basic question here is not one of our *knowledge* of Jesus as the Christ. The basic question is a question about the *reality* of "Jesus as the Christ." And that reality came about through God's creative and elective action of Israel throughout her generations until Jesus of Nazareth emerged out of Israel as the Christ—of God and of Israel. This discloses why the church needs the Old Testament no less than the New, until it reaches that point beyond history when it needs neither.

But someone may reply, "Exactly. When Jesus fulfils something of the Old Testament that something comes to an *end*. It is superseded and left behind, and should be forgotten." Such a view is a profound misunderstanding. The New Testament's fulfilment of the Old Testament does not mean that the Old Testament comes to an end and is to be forgotten since there is nothing left. On the contrary, the Old Testament is brought to an end in the sense that it arises again, in its New form, the form of the Resurrection, that is, of eternal life.

If the Old came to an absolute end, the cross would be the last word. But the Old comes to an end in a grave out of which—and not from somewhere else!—arises the Resurrection. The sin, judgment, and death of the Old can come to an end indeed. But out of death comes life, out of judgment salvation, out of sin the righteousness of God displayed in the gospel. For the "testament" of the Old Testament is not a testament of sin and death but of the grace of God that overcomes sin and death. The Old Testament is also a form of the gospel. The Old Testament, the covenant of God, arises again, for the blood of Jesus is the blood of the *new* covenant (Luke 22:20). If the Old Testament had come to an end in some other sense than that of biblical eschatology—for example, in some secular sense in which death is regarded as the final end—the Christian church would have eliminated the Old Testament. But that is not the case. The Old Testament is needed not simply as an aid to our understanding. The notion that it is, lies behind our misunderstanding that the election of Jesus by God as the Christ is wholly intelligible within a forgetting of the election of Israel; and similarly, it lies behind our misunderstanding that the nature of the church can be understood without reference to Israel.

It is true that nothing new emerges in the New Testament that was not contained in the Old. As Augustine said, what the New Testament reveals is concealed in the Old Testament. But it is not merely *concealed* in the Old, it is ontologically grounded in the Old and inextricably bound up with it. To attempt to have what the New contains apart from and as something other than the New form of the Old, is to divorce what belongs together.

Let us consider one of the aspects of Israel's reality that was actualized and fulfilled in Christ. Israel was summoned by God to a life of faith and obedience that would demonstrate her divine election and covenant status before the eyes of the world. Her very existence and style of life was to be prophetic, a proclamation of Yahweh to all other nations. But Israel often failed to live according to her calling. She violated her covenant, forsook Yahweh, sought after false gods, worshiped idols, despised the fatherless, sold the poor for a pair of shoes, forsook the widow, trampled on the weak, oppressed those who had no defense. Then God would raise up a prophet, who would call Israel back to God and to the ways of the covenant, because by her sinful disloyalty to

Yahweh's name he was obscured and even evil spoken of among the nations.

Israel did not send missionaries to the pagan nations. This has often perplexed Christians. God raised up prophets (Jonah being the exception) from within Israel to speak his word to Israel. For Israel by her very existence had to embody the word of Yahweh; her religious, social, economic, national, and international life had itself to be a proclamation of the truth of Yahweh's covenant with Israel, that all nations might see the wonder of Israel's God and know that there is none like him.

Jesus came out of this prophetic tradition. He fulfilled the prophetic function of Israel's election. He accomplished what Israel failed to do. At the beginning of his public ministry Jesus identified himself and described his task, "The Spirit of the Lord is upon me, because he has anointed me to preach good news to the poor. He has sent me to proclaim release to the captives and recovering of sight to the blind, to set at liberty those who are oppressed, to proclaim the acceptable year of the Lord"; and then Jesus adds: "Today this Scripture has been fulfilled in your hearing" (Luke 4:18-21). As the fulfilment of Israel's prophetic function, he was also the end of it. Jesus became what the church came to call him, Jesus the Christ, our chief prophet, who fully revealed in his person and work the word of God, the truth about Yahweh that could thereafter only be echoed and repeated, but not superseded.

The ancient prophets of Israel spoke God's word. But they acknowledged that they were not themselves the prophetic word. They often began their oracles, "Thus says the Lord," and frequently they declared that the word of the Lord was on them—as a burden on an animal. Jesus, however, never said, "Thus says the Lord"; instead he introduced his words with "But I say unto you," and he did so even in contradiction of Israel's religious tradition. Jesus never declared that the word of the Lord was "on him." He never regarded it as a burden on his back, as something other than himself. Instead he claimed, I am the Truth, the Life, the Way, the Light of the world, the true Bread from heaven, the true Shepherd.

Not only did Israel fail to be the nation God had called her to be; she also failed to listen to her prophets and, worse, she often killed those sent to her by God. In the end Israel also killed Jesus for fulfilling the task and function of her election. Through the event of the cross, Jesus, within Israel and for Israel, became the concrete form and historical reality of God's word to the world. Through the cross he revealed the name and glory of Yahweh to all nations. Thus Jesus became the ultimate fulfilment of Israel's election to be a sign of Yahweh's covenantal grace to all peoples. In Jesus the prophet and the word are identical. By identifying himself with Israel's election, Jesus became God's Elect and could claim that he himself was "the way, the truth, and the life." He is the way, the truth, the life, because he *became* these through his identification and actualization of Israel's prophetic task. Had he not fulfilled Israel's election and perfectly rendered the service it demanded, he would not be the way, the truth, and the life, the Christ of God, the one in whom God is well pleased.

*   *   *

In fulfilling Israel's election, Jesus reveals fully the nature of that election and thereby the nature of God's intent and purpose in it. God's election of Israel is not countered or restrictively limited by a corresponding rejection of Israel. Nor does God elect Israel to be a blessing to all the nations of the earth and also a curse to all—or even to some—of them. God's whole and unqualified intent and purpose in electing Israel is the redemption of Israel and through Israel the redemption of the world. This redemptively elective purpose of God is profoundly distorted by the notion of a decree that defines God's purpose and intent in terms of "whatsoever comes to pass." Israel's election reveals that God's single and only purpose and intent with Israel is redemptive and gracious.

This purpose is fully revealed in God's election of Jesus as the Christ. The writer of the Fourth Gospel says it plainly: "God so loved the world that he gave his only Son, that whoever believes in him should not perish but have eternal life." The Evangelist does not add—as decretal theology might, under the aegis of "whatsoever comes to pass"—that God also sent his Son so that whoever does not believe might be damned. On the contrary, the writer immediately fore-stalls such an idea by declaring that "God sent the Son into the world, not to condemn the world, but that the world might be saved through him" (John 3:17). God's single purpose in sending Christ is redemptive, and this fully reveals and fulfils the divine intent of the election of Israel. God's purpose in his election of Israel is not "in the same manner," nor indeed, in any decree or manner, revealed in his nonelec-tion or reprobation of ancient Egypt or ancient Moab. Nor is God's election of Jesus as the Christ in any degree contingent on, or in any sense involved in or unavoidably enmeshed, logically or otherwise, with the rejection of anything *outside of himself* in his status as God's Elect. God's whole purpose and intent lies in and is explicated by Jesus Christ, *our Lord.*

The truth of this can be indicated in two ways. First, if God's election of Israel necessarily involves, either as a pre-condition or as a result, the rejection of other nations, then it is not a wholly free election. If God cannot elect Israel without thereby necessarily rejecting other nations, his elec-tion of Israel is bound by its consequences. In such a case, all Gentile nations would by Israel's election be unavoidably reprobate. But a God who cannot elect without thereby reprobating nations or individuals is not a free and sovereign God.

Reformed theology rejects Arminianism because it makes God comply with *human* conditions. It rejects the notions that God is not free to operate except within conditions laid down by man and that God cannot save man unless man first decides to believe and choose God. But when Reformed theology rejects Arminian theology by an appeal to the human logic of rationality, and argues that God is governed by these laws of logic, Reformed theology merely substitutes the laws of logic and rationality for the Arminian's decision. Along this route Reformed theology can never displace Ar-minian theology. Such a substitution is neither adequate nor helpful. The answer to the Arminian's imposition of restric-tions on God is not the imposition of the necessity of logical consequence on him. It is as erroneous to impose inevitable logical consequences on God's elective action as it is to condition it on man's choice. God's elective act is as free of the one as of the other. God's election of Israel and his election of Christ are wholly free. This free character of election stems from the wholly free character of divine grace. Election is always gracious and therefore never loses the freedom that belongs to the essence of divine grace. Every attempt by decretal theology to encapsulate reprobation within election, every attempt to include "whatsoever comes to pass" within God's gracious "eternal purpose which he has realized in Christ Jesus our Lord" (Eph. 3:11) is destructive of its wholly free and gracious character.

How exactly Christ fulfils Israel's prophetic function! Israel's prophets were not missionaries. They addressed themselves to Israel and to the nations of their times through their word to Israel. Nor was Jesus himself a missionary.[4] He declared to a Canaanite woman that he was sent only to the lost sheep of the house of Israel, and that it was not fair to give the children's food to the dogs (Matt. 15:21ff.). These words are strange to people who think of Jesus as a missionary sent to the Gentiles. And all the attempts to escape the force of these strange words by suggesting that Jesus' remark was only meant to test this woman's faith are clearly a dodge. But these words lose their strangeness if we recognize that Jesus fulfilled the task for which God had elected Israel.

Paul explicitly speaks of this restricted function of Jesus when he says, "For I tell you that Christ became a servant to the circumcised to show God's truthfulness, in order to confirm the promises given to the patriarchs, and in order that the Gentiles might glorify God for his mercy" (Rom. 15:8f.). Paul then defines this in terms of the Old Testament by adding, "As it is written, Therefore I will praise thee among the Gentiles, and sing to thy name" (vs. 9). Paul contrasts himself with Jesus. While Christ "became a servant to the circumcised," grace was given to Paul "to be a minister of Christ Jesus to the Gentiles" (vs. 16). The move to the

---

4 Precisely because Jesus was no missionary, but more than one, the church cannot be defined as mission. The existential remark, "The church is mission," is theologically inept and confusing. The church is more than mission because election as a divine creative action is more than a mere summons to service.

Gentiles came through Paul. Jesus fulfilled only Israel's peculiar calling and task as regards the Gentiles; hence, Paul proves that Jesus' ministry was a service to the circumcised.

Jesus' election is the fulfilment and meaning and actualization of Israel's election. It occurs as a movement within Israel's election, which threads its way through Isaac who displaces Ishmael, through Jacob who displaces Esau, through the tribe of Judah to the exclusion of the other tribes, through David who displaces Saul, through Solomon who alone carries the crown rights of David's son, through the two tribes that return from Babylon as a remnant representing the twelve tribes until the line narrows on Jesus born of a virgin betrothed to Joseph.

Jesus' election does not imply that all other Israelites are reprobates, although at the end of the narrowing process Jesus stands alone as God's Elect. Jesus fulfils Israel's election; he does not annihilate it. His election no more implies the reprobation of the nation of Israel than the election of Israel meant the reprobation of the Gentile nations. The election of Jesus, on the contrary, is inextricably related to the election of Israel. For there is no election of Jesus without the election of Israel, and no election of Israel which is not the election of Jesus as the Christ, no more than Jesus can be the seed of Abraham without Abraham. The reality of the one is involved in the reality of the other.

We have considered one of the prophetic facets of Israel's election and indicated how it was fully actualized and fulfilled in Christ. It could also be shown how the priesthood and kingship of Israel became wholly actualized in the person of Jesus Christ through God's elective and creative action. The distinction between priest and offering is overcome in Christ, who is both the priest and the lamb of sacrifice. The entire movement of thought in the Epistle to the Hebrews concerns Jesus' superiority to the angels, to Moses, to Joshua, and to the Levitical priesthood, because he is a priest after the order of Melchizedek; and hence his once-for-all sacrifice is the fulfilment and actualization of Israel's election as a nation of priests. Concerning Jesus' status as our only High Priest, the writer says that "one does not take the honor upon himself, but he is called by God, just as Aaron was. So also Christ did not exalt himself to be made a high priest, but was appointed by him who said to him, 'Thou art my Son, this day have I begotten thee' " (Heb. 5:4f.). If, indeed, the divine begetting of Jesus, as Hebrews teaches, was itself God's election of Jesus to be the great High Priest, how could Jesus have elected himself to the honor of his priesthood? Such action would have presupposed his existence, whereas the thought in Hebrews is that his election is a matter of his existence. Christ's election by God to fulfil the priesthood to which Israel was elected is strikingly clear.

It could also be shown that the kingship to which Israel was called was fulfilled in Christ, in whom the king and the kingdom are identical, so that when the king is present in the world the kingdom is also present. As the kings of Israel were representatives of the whole people—hence the history of the kingdom of Israel is written in terms of her kings (I and II Kings, I and II Chronicles)—so Christ as king represents the whole of Israel and recapitulates the whole history of Israel in his own life. It is enough here to note that the movement in each instance is similar to that movement in which the prophetic aspect of Israel's calling received concrete embodiment and fulfilment in Jesus as the Christ.

A similar movement of actualization could be traced as God's covenant with Israel takes on its new and full form in Christ whose blood is the blood of the new covenant; or as the temple finally emerges in Christ, in whom the godhead dwells bodily, a temple that can be cast down and built again in three days. The movement is always an elective, creative, divine action within Israel and its history that culminates in its fulness in Jesus as the Christ.

The parallels between God's elective, creative action that produced Abraham and his seed Israel and the similar divine action that produced Immanuel in Bethlehem are indeed remarkable. Abraham was impotent; Joseph had no father-role to play. Sarah was beyond child-bearing age; Mary was a virgin. There was no Israel in Abraham and Sarah; the nation of Israel at the time of Jesus' birth was a religious wasteland that had gone without prophecy for hundreds of years, a politically occupied country under the rule of Rome. Jesus truly emerged as a tender plant out of the dry ground. As

Abraham gets a son by divine miracle, Israel by a divine creative action gets Jesus out of virgin soil; but Jesus emerges not indeed apart from, but from within Mary when the Almighty comes upon this virgin and in the shadow begets the son of his election. As with Israel, so with Jesus. Each has its reality in the elective and creative action of God.

*   *   *

The election of Jesus is seldom expressed in the Gospels, yet it is in the background almost everywhere. Many of the disputes between the Jews and Jesus turned on the question of his right to do what he did. Most involved the question, "By what authority [do] you do these things?" (Luke 20:2). Jesus' authority rested in his election by God to judge the religious life and institutions of Israel and to be and proclaim their truth.

Nonetheless the election of Jesus is explicitly expressed at the crucial points in his life. The declaration from the heavens at Jesus' baptism, "Thou art my beloved Son; with thee I am well pleased" (Luke 3:22), was public declaration of his peculiar status before God and of the distinctiveness that set him apart from all others. The same affirmation was made on the Mount of Transfiguration, where Jesus was assured of his continuity with Moses and Elijah. According to Luke, the affirmation was made in words that spoke explicitly of Christ's election: "This is my Son, my Chosen; listen to him" (Luke 9:35). For the Gospel writers, "in thee I am well pleased," "thou art my beloved Son," and "my Son, my Chosen" are only varying ways of saying that Jesus is God's Elect. These declarations distinguish Jesus from all his Jewish contemporaries. Though the Jews are an elect people, though they are the son that God called out of Egypt, though they are loved by God, these affirmations concerning Jesus publicly demonstrate how peculiar and unique Jesus' election is. They are reminiscent of God's assertion "Behold my servant, whom I uphold, my chosen, in whom my soul delights" (Isa. 42:1), words that distinguish between elect Israel and one who is peculiarly God's servant and God's choice.

The Jews so understood them. Modern Christians may

have forgotten the nature of the issue that ended in the mockery that took place at the foot of the cross. The Jews at least knew the name of the issue. Moreover, it is clear from New Testament usage of terms like "Son of God," the "one in whom God delights," "the king of Israel" that they were used interchangeably. According to Matthew's account of the crucifixion the Jews derided Jesus because he claimed to be "the King of the Jews" and "the Son of God." In their mockery they say, "He trusts in God; let God deliver him now, *if he desires him*" (Matt. 27:43). To be the King of the Jews was to be the Son of God, and to be both of these was to be one whom God *desired*. To be the Christ was to be God's chosen. Even in Hebrews, as noted above, the phrase "Thou art my Son, today I have begotten thee" is adduced as proof that Jesus did not take honor to himself but that God elected him the great High Priest. Again, Peter in his Pentecost sermon declared that God made Jesus, whom the Jews had crucified, "to be both Lord and Christ" (Acts 2:36). Thus the election of Christ appears sometimes implicitly and often explicitly in the various titles the New Testament ascribes to him.

Taken all in all God's election of Jesus as the Christ receives extensive and profoundly significant affirmation in the New Testament. This should not be surprising. If Jesus is the fulfilment of Israel's election, the election of Jesus in its New Testament fulfilment should be at least as conspicuous in the New Testament as the election of Israel is in the Old Testament.

Clearly in biblical thought Israel and Jesus' election are inseparably interrelated. Christ's election in its reality is involved in the very substance of Israel's election, and Israel's election is not merely an example of Christ's election given for pedagogical reasons that may be dismissed. It would be better to assert that the interrelationship is symbolic, in the profound sense in which the symbol is itself an expression of the reality it symbolizes because it participates in it. Thus the election of Israel is symbolic of Jesus' election—the Old Testament form of the reality of Jesus' election; and the election of Jesus is symbolic of Israel's election—the New Testament form of its reality.

Has not something central in the New Testament been lost when the church preaches Jesus Christ as though it were proclaiming someone quite like the rest of us, with a first and a last name, and rarely indicates that "Christ" means that Jesus is God's Elect? Does not such preaching ignore a mighty weapon against "Christian" antisemitism? And does it not unwittingly, but nonetheless actually, permit the church to forget that its origin lies in the fact that *salvation is of the Jews?*

CHAPTER VIII

The Election of the Church

The church is a thing of mystery. Its mystery stems from what Paul refers to as "the mystery of Christ" (Eph. 3:4). Paul asserts that this mystery "was not made known to the sons of men in other generations as it has now been revealed to his holy apostles and prophets by the Spirit" (vs. 5). What is the mystery of Christ? "How the Gentiles are fellow heirs, members of the same body, and partakers of the promise in Christ Jesus through the gospel" (vs. 6). By the grace of God Paul was made a minister of this mystery to the Gentiles "to make all men see what is the plan of the mystery hidden for ages in God who created all things; that through the church the manifold wisdom of God might now be made known to the principalities and the powers in the heavenly places. This was according to the eternal purpose which he has realized in Christ Jesus our Lord" (vv. 9-11).

This is a rich biblical deposit of truth about the church. The mystery of the church derives from the mystery of Christ, namely, that God in his wisdom eternally purposed in Christ that the Gentiles should become heirs and partakers of all the spiritual blessings that belong to Israel by virtue of her election. The actualization of this mysterious eternal purpose in Christ, through the gospel, creates the church, so that the wisdom of God, who created all things, might through the existence of the church be made known to the principalities and powers in the heavenly places.

This mystery of the church was not wholly unknown in

former generations. The Old Testament does speak of Israel as a blessing to all the nations of the earth, and of Abraham as the father of many nations. Yet from these suggestive affirmations the emergence of the church could not be deduced. What prevented such deductions was the fact of Israel's exclusive election by God. She alone, and no Gentile nation, was elect. Hence the mystery of Christ also lay athwart such a process of logical inference, for the mystery of Christ is disclosed in that creative action of Christ's death, whereby he created of Jew and Gentile that one new humanity which is the church. The inference of the election of a church containing Gentiles from Israel's election faced a gap that only the creative power of Christ's death could fill (see Eph. 2:11ff.). Israel's election was something she could not share with other nations. God himself had assured her of her peculiar relation to himself. It took the creative act of Christ's death to make Gentiles heirs and partakers of Israel's election.

The church at Ephesus did not understand this and therefore understood neither herself nor Paul. Having set forth the mystery of the church, Paul says to the Ephesians, "So I ask you not to lose heart over what I am suffering for you, which is your glory" (Eph. 3:13). To this we must return.

In Colossians, another facet of this long-hidden mystery is discussed. Christ is presented as the first-born of all creation, the one in whom and through whom and for whom all things were created (1:16). In Christ all things are said to consist, and "in him all the fulness of God was pleased to dwell, and through him to reconcile to himself all things" (1:19). The church according to the letter to the Ephesians is Christ's body, "the fulness of him who fills all in all" (1:23). To this connection between Christ as the cosmic focal point and Christ as the head of the church we must also return.

Finally, in Romans, especially in chapters 10 and 11, Paul speaks of Israel's advantage over the Gentiles, of Israel's election, and of Israel's unbelief through which the Gentiles come to share in Israel's election and in all that Israel's election means. To this too we must return.

Before we return to these topics, let us look at what Christian theology has done throughout history with the

election of the church. Just as it has never denied the election
of Israel or the election of Christ, Christian thought has never
denied that the church is the object of God's election. But
here, too, little has been made of it. When Berkhof, for
example, discusses the objects of election, he does not even
mention the church. He does raise the matter of election in
connection with the church in his discussion of what the
church is. The church is said to be the "community of the
elect" *(coetus electorum)*. But Berkhof is not at all happy
with this definition. It defines the church, he says, ideally—as
it exists as an idea in God—but not as it exists in history,
which for any Reformed person comprises believers and their
seed, not all of whom become believers.

The church as the "community of the elect"—as Augustine
and others were prone to define it—more defines the community in terms of its individual elect members than it points to
an elect community. It leaves open the crucial question as to
how elect individuals do in fact constitute an elect community. Is the church as a corporate community, as a body, the
object of election? Can we speak of an elect church, or only
of elect individual members?

According to biblical thought, it seems that individual
election does not do justice to the election of the church.
John addresses his second epistle to "the elect lady and her
children" and closes with "The children of your elect sister
greet you" (2 John 1, 13). Moreover, the individual elect
Christian in biblical thought is always seen as a member of
the body. As a pure individual he has no status in the church.
He is always more than his individual self; he is a member of
what is more than himself, the church. It is this view that is
presupposed in the Reformed doctrine of infant baptism. The
infant, one of the Reformed baptismal formularies declares,
"as a member of Christ's church ought to be baptized." The
crucial question is how to retain the corporate, community
aspect of the church if the church is defined as a "community of the elect."

To define the church in this way differs little from defining it as "the number of the elect." Indeed, Berkhof on the
one hand dislikes "community of the elect" as a definition of
the church because some elect are as yet unborn. Yet, on the

other hand, he concedes that it is an ideal definition of the church as it exists as idea in the mind of God. Both what Berkhof likes and what he dislikes about defining the church as "community of the elect" relate to *number*. The attempt to define the church in terms of elected individuals always becomes in the end a definition of the church in terms of the *number* of the elect. And this does not define the church as an elect community, for the number of the church is only one. There is but *one* holy, catholic church, and the church is defined not by number but by unity.

The tendency to define the election of the church in terms of the number of its elect members surfaces in other areas of Reformed thought as well. The Canons of Dort speak of the "number of the elect," and declare that this number can neither be enlarged or decreased. This made good sense as a disclaimer against Arminian theology, according to which the number of the elect is determined by man. But defining election in terms of number is dangerous. Number implies limitation, and the idea that limitation determined the nature of election soon gave rise to the idea that election would be something other than it is if God were to elect all men![1] This is untenable. Election is what it is whether it has few men, many men, or all men, as its object. To make number, in the context of *individual* election, an essential feature of election is to make reprobation an inherent quality of election. When this happens both ideas become blurred and ultimately indistinguishable. Defining election in terms of number also gave rise to the idea that election is a basis from which one can deduce reprobation by logical consequence and mathematical necessity. If, indeed, number, a highly abstract concept, is of the essence of election, election itself becomes so highly abstract that reprobation becomes congenital to election, and a single definition can serve to define both. But if we continue down this route, everything becomes so vague as to be interchangeable. We have seen how Hoeksema reversed the order and made reprobation the precondition of election. For

[1] This method, interestingly, has often been followed in defining the nature of grace. Henri Rondet says, "Whether they were Congruists, Molinists, or Banezians, theologians all presupposed that if grace were given to all men, it would no longer be grace." *The Grace of Christ*, p. 334.

him the logic of reprobation is election. If Reformed theology can accept both that the logic of election is reprobation and the logic of reprobation election, it has accepted another form of the "in the same manner" that the Canons of Dort explicitly reject. Hoeksema's reversal took place in such rarefied atmosphere that only G. C. Berkouwer seems to have been greatly disturbed by it.[2] But a concept of election in which number is essential is so abstract that a decretal theologian can soon completely eliminate the concept of number and contend that there is but a single decree in which such distinctions as number exist only for our finite, conditioned way of thinking.

Number has also played a role in other areas of Reformed theology. The grace of God became special, saving grace, something for the elect only, since it saves only the elect. Along the same route, the infinite nature of Christ's atoning death turned into a doctrine of limited atonement, with few questions asked and none permitted.[3]

All of these attempts to employ number—the idea of limitation—to understand the nature of election, the election of the church, the nature of divine grace, and of Christ's atonement are really attempts to reduce the mystery of Christian truths to boundaries that we can rationally manage. Down this road all mystery disappears—the mystery of unbelief and no less the mystery of Christ and of the church.

If one approaches the election of the church in terms of the number of the elect, the church's election constitutes no special problem or mystery. Nor is there any point in asking whether the church is essentially a Jewish phenomenon, or a Gentile phenomenon, or a Jewish *and* Gentile phenomenon. But once the church is simply equated with the elect regarded as number, and the mysterious has been cleared away, much of the rich and complex New Testament teaching

[2] *Divine Election,* p. 207.

[3] It was along this route that the explicit teaching of the Canons of Dort about the infinite nature of Christ's atonement came to be designated as a teaching of "limited atonement." So remarkable a doctrine would surely have called for scriptural demonstration, yet the Canons cite no Scripture passages to prove "limited atonement."

about the church becomes inconsequential. From the biblical perspective, however, particularly from the perspective of Israel's unique election, the inclusion of the Gentiles within the church is surprising and remarkable, a mystery that required a special New Testament revelation by the Spirit.

The church that took shape with the coming of the Holy Spirit on Pentecost was a wholly Jewish church. The amazement that the gospel was also for the Gentiles and the stubborn reluctance of the Jerusalem church to accept this are familiar. The Jerusalem church tried to reduce this new phenomenon into something more palatable by the demand that Gentile Christians become Jewish Christians. The Jewish church for some time insisted that the church was for Jews only. It required a transformation of their theology to rid them of this idea. When they finally acknowledged that Gentiles could also share in the salvation wrought by Israel's Messiah, they knew something new had happened. And it was Paul who gave them a new understanding of the church by disclosing the mystery of the church.

*   *   *

Paul's Epistle to the Ephesians is about Christ and the church. It begins with a rich description of Christ that portrays him as one whom God had raised from the dead, placed at his right hand, and given dominion to subject all things under his feet. As such, Christ is the head of the church, and the church is defined as the fulness of Christ.

From this description of the person and function of Christ, Paul proceeds directly to describe the Ephesian Christians. They had been separated from the Jews by a wide chasm. They were at first children of wrath, "separated from Christ, alienated from the commonwealth of Israel, and strangers to the covenants of promise, having no hope and without God in the world" (2:12). That is exactly how Israel and the Jewish church at Jerusalem saw the Gentiles; and they did not spontaneously drop this point of view even after Gentiles became Christians.

Indeed, that is what Gentile Christians—all of them—once

were. Paul asks the Gentile church at Ephesus—even as Christians and members of the church—not to forget this. Something had happened to change things, but they had to remember how it was before in order to appreciate how it became afterward.

What had happened occurred in the death of Christ. The separation of Jew and Gentile and the enmity that lay in this separation had been overcome. It had been subjected by Christ to Christ through his death on the cross. Christ had broken down the wall of separation. In his death he reconciled both Jew and Gentile to God and created of the two one new humanity, the church, which is then characterized not by number but by *unity*. What separated the Gentile from the Jew was the barrier of "the law of commandments and ordinances" (Eph. 2:15) that was part of Israel's religious heritage. This Christ abolished "in his flesh," that is, by his death, thus replacing the enmity between the two by peace. In this way he became the head of the church and created in himself that one new humanity which is the church and the *mystery* of the church.

This is the new thing that happened, the mystery of Christ that remained hidden for generations, the mystery of the church. The distinctive feature of the church is its inclusion of the Gentiles. This feature of the church did not come to expression on Pentecost or in the early Jewish church in Jerusalem. But this feature of the church is grounded in Christ's death on the cross, on which Pentecost itself depended. And this distinctive, surprising, and mysterious feature of the church is completely filtered out when the church is defined simply as the community or number of the elect. The exclusive feature of God's election of the nation of Israel, together with the inclusion of Gentiles in the church, belongs inherently and inextricably to the election of the church. It should be observed that the grounding of the church in Christ's death was a *creative* act. "We," says Paul, "are his workmanship, created in Christ Jesus" (Eph. 2:10), for the purpose of Christ's death "was that he might *create* in himself one new man in place of two" (vs. 15).

The election of the church is not defined in terms of the

election of individuals with a direct, ahistorical reference to eternity. The assertion that individuals are elected from eternity is not in itself false. But it is a largely empty and abstract assertion unless it is uttered within, and takes its content and resonance from, the rich biblical context about election. When Paul deals with the election of Israel and the salvation of the Gentiles and the complex relation between the two, he is not talking about an abstract, faceless, characterless individual election. For Paul the election of the Jewish people is a very Jewish datum. It is as Jewish as Jesus and as real as the truth Jesus uttered to the Samaritan woman: "Salvation is from the Jews" (John 4:22).

This unifying and reconciling of Jew and Gentile wrought by Christ through his death, which issues in the creation of the church, becomes a concrete sign and reflection in history of Christ's cosmic task of uniting all things. Colossians suggests many disunities of things in heaven and on earth, of things visible and invisible. Paul asserts that it is the Father's pleasure that in Christ all the cosmic fulness should dwell and that Christ, through the blood of his cross, should reconcile all things to himself, in order that he may have the preeminence in all things. This reconcilation of all things in Christ is inextricably related to Christ as the head of the church and to the church as the fulness of Christ. We cannot discuss here this complex and rich truth about Christ. The point is that unless we recognize this new, reconciling, creative event that occurred in the death of Christ and issued in the creation of the church, we lack the biblical perspective from which to understand Christ's work of cosmic reconciliation and unification. Paul's letter to the Colossians shows that the cosmic Christ, who has preeminence in all things, cannot be understood apart from his death, by which he reconciled and united Jew and Gentile and created the church.

*   *   *

The election of Israel and its relation to the salvation of Gentiles is nowhere more fully discussed than in Romans 10 and 11. To this we now turn.

In Romans 10 Paul discusses the unbelief of Israel. The

Jews had sought to achieve their own righteousness through the law and did not subject themselves to the righteousness of God, which is Christ. They did not heed the gospel. Paul proves this by quoting Isaiah. They had indeed heard it, as Paul shows by quoting Psalm 19:4. And they understood it, as Paul indicates by quoting Moses and Isaiah. Paul ends the tenth chapter by quoting what God said through Isaiah, "All day long I have held out my hands to a disobedient and contrary people."

It is significant that all the proofs Paul adduces to show that the Jewish nation rejected Christ come from the Old Testament. Of course, Paul had no other Scripture to quote, but he might have appealed to Israel's rejection of the gospel in the form in which it was present in the life of Christ, and as it was preached to them after the Cross and Resurrection. Instead, he demonstrates Israel's unbelief and rejection of Christ by an appeal to descriptions of Old Testament Israel given by men dating back as far as Moses, in whose days Israel first acquired national structure and form. Two things are evident here.

First, Paul sees the Israel of his day as the Israel of old. Israel's unbelief in Christ was no different from its unbelief in the days of Moses and Isaiah. When Paul, therefore, begins Chapter 11 with the question, "Has God rejected his people?" and answers it "By no means!", he is closing the door on the position that God is finished with the nation of Israel because the Jews rejected Christ as he came to them in the early proclamation of the apostles. Earlier in Romans (3:3), Paul has asked, "What if some were unfaithful? Does their faithlessness nullify the faithfulness of God?" Paul does not specify there *what* they did not believe, but it makes no difference as regards the faithfulness of God to his election of Israel. No kind of unbelief can undo and evaporate God's faithful commitment to his election and promise to Israel. Hence no form of unbelief on the part of Israel can be employed as an argument to support the contention that God has cast off the nation Israel.

Second, it is clear that the inclusion of the Gentiles within salvation does not displace the Jewish nation. The salvation of the Gentiles depends in fact on continued divine acceptance of Israel, and on the lasting quality of Israel's election. Put differently: the church does not displace Israel; on the contrary, the very reality of the church depends on the truth that God has not cast off Israel. And the religious health of the church depends on its recognizing that its existence depends on God's faithfulness to Israel, as does its ultimate understanding of itself and the purpose of its existence.[4]

The idea that the church is a Gentile institution, a substitute for and displacement of Israel as a nation, is a profound misunderstanding both of God's election of Israel and of the church itself. In reality, it is only the reverse of the misunderstanding that obtained in the early New Testament church, which contended that Gentile Christians had to become Christian Jews. Gentiles need not become Christian Jews; nor must Jews now become Christian *Gentiles.* The church will fulfil its mission to the Jews when—in God's own time—it becomes the kind of church that provokes unbelieving Israel to anger and jealousy because it makes apparent by its confession and life that it is nothing in itself and that whatever it is and possesses derives from the religious resources of Israel. For the church is nothing and has nothing that it has not received from the religious treasure that God gave to Israel. Not until the church acknowledges this will it fulfil its own purpose, its mission to Israel.

In chapter 11 what Paul hints at in chapter 10 is explicitly urged. He begins against the background of chapter 10 by asking whether God has cast off his people. His emphatic answer is No. The remainder of the chapter is devoted to a substantiation of that No. To begin with, he himself is an Israelite, of the seed of Abraham, of the tribe of Benjamin. As a Christian, then, he is evidence that God has not cast off the nation of Israel.

The meaning of nation in this context is crucial. Theological traditions that operate with only a doctrine of individual election urge that nation refers simply to the number of individual elect Jews, and that God's not casting off his

---

[4] For a further statement of the unbreakable connection between Israel and the church, see Jacob Jocz, *A Theology of Election,* p. 134.

people means simply that God has not cast off any of these individual elect Jews. But the question whether God casts off individual elect Jews is not even on the horizon of Paul's thought. If it were, his later remarks about Jewish branches being cut off and cast aside and about the possibility, if they do not continue in unbelief, of being engrafted again, would have obscured and confused his whole concern. Paul's question is a far more difficult one, as the complexity of his answer shows. It is whether God has cast off the nation as a corporate, historical reality.

For Paul the sum of the number of individual elect Jews is not the nation. He points to himself and to the seven thousand non-Baal worshipers in Israel at the time of Elijah, and urges that both are tokens of God's not having rejected Israel. To be sure, some Jews were hardened and did not obtain the righteousness of God through faith. But this does not prompt God to cast off the nation. This is the argument of Romans 3 all over again. Lack of faith on the part of some does not void the faithfulness of God. No amount of unbelief on Israel's part can dissolve God's election of his people.

It is not the elect, believing, individual Jews—the small remnant—that constitute the nation of Israel; rather they serve the function of a remnant by being a token of the nation as a whole. The element that runs through the entire discussion is this: while God uses the unbelief of the Jews, God does not dissolve his election of Israel by casting them off, for, as Paul indicates at the end of chapter 11, God's gifts and calling are irrevocable.

Some, Paul says in the second place, were indeed hardened. They stumbled. They fell. "A hardening has come upon part of Israel" (vs. 25). Even this was not an end in itself, but it occurred for the sake of the salvation of the Gentiles. Again, we hark back to Romans 3, where Paul asserts that God uses Jewish unbelief to display the truth that his faithfulness endures nonetheless. Far from undoing God's faithfulness, Israel's faithlessness only demonstrates its greatness and persistence; and God uses Israel's faithlessness to bring salvation to the Gentiles and to provoke unbelieving Israel to jealousy of that salvation which belonged to her but through her unbelief went to the Gentiles. The very movement of

God to the Gentiles is made to provoke the Jewish nation to a jealousy that will reclaim its loss of that which made the Gentiles rich. The Gentiles are not saved merely for their own sake, but for the sake of God's election of Israel. How unshakable is the faithfulness of God to the nation he has chosen!

Paul's third point is that if Israel's impoverishment works the enrichment of the world, how much more will Israel's fulness enrich the world. If, says Paul, the casting away of Israel is the reconciliation of the world, what shall the receiving of them be but life from death. Israel's return, her fulness, will be for the world like a resurrection from the dead! Paul's whole description of this movement of God—from Israel to the Gentiles and through Gentile-provoked jealousy to Israel's fulness, and back again to the world—powerfully underscores God's faithfulness to Israel and to his promise that Israel will be a blessing to all nations. This movement of God's elective grace through history is not a straight path. Its route turns out from itself toward the Gentiles and then back inward upon itself and then out again toward the whole world. Such a movement defies ordinary logic, and cannot be grasped by any rationally predictable processes of inference or deduction. In fact, it renders all neatly packaged logical systems suspect. This does not mean that God's grace and election are irrational, merely that the "logic" of grace and election goes beyond human rationality.

Fourth, Paul argues that if the dough offered as firstfruits is holy, the whole lump is holy, and if the root is holy, so are the branches. If some Israelites believed, the mass of Israel is also holy, for there could be no holy firstfruits of the lump unless the lump were itself holy. Here Paul is arguing from the particular (the firstfruits) to the general (the lump). Then he goes on to say that if the root is holy, so are the branches, for there could be no holy branches unless the root were holy. Now he is arguing from the general (the root) to the particulars (the branches). In other words, the whole involves the individual and the individual involves the whole.

The lump and the root are Israel as God's elect nation. From the perspective of the New Testament (though Paul's perspective throughout is in terms of the Old Testament), the

lump and the root are Christ. For Paul's argument it makes
no *essential* difference, for the lump or root is holy by virtue
of God's faithful and unchanging election of Israel, which in
its highest form is Christ.

Paul's fifth point is addressed to Gentile Christians. If
some of the branches were broken off, and the Gentiles, as
wild olives, were engrafted among the natural branches, they
ought not on that account become proud and boastful over
against the broken-off branches. As an engrafted branch, the
Gentiles live off the olive tree (Israel). Paul tells the Gentile
Christians to remember that they are eating from Israel's
table and sharing in her covenant, election, and Messiah. And
Paul tells them not to say that Jewish branches were broken
off because of their unbelief. This is true, but the Gentiles
cannot forget that they have their present status by faith. If
God broke off the natural branches because of unbelief,
surely the engrafted ones have no warranty that they cannot
be broken off.

The Gentiles need to bear in mind that, in the light of
Israel's election, the engrafting of Gentiles into participation
in Israel's riches and status before God is *unnatural.* This is
the mystery of Christ and the mystery of the church: what
could not naturally occur, from the viewpoint of Israel's
unique and exclusive election, did occur.

From this it is plain that the Gentiles participate in Israel's
election and all those treasures of religious promises and
blessings that go with it. The Gentiles have neither election,
nor covenant, nor law, nor Messiah of their own. Salvation is
of the Jews. This is no temporary, passing fact. It remains
ever true that the Gentiles have no gospel of their own, only
a gospel that is for the Jew first, and only then also for the
Gentile. Israel's election gave the Jew the advantage. And
even though the Jews no less than the Gentiles were under
condemnation because of their sin, the Jew still has an
advantage. The sin of the Jews did not destroy their privileged status before God, because it could not destroy his
faithful commitment to his gifts and election of Israel.

That is why Gentile Christians may not boast over against
the branches broken off. For the Christian church to believe
that the church is "in" and unbelieving Israel is "out" would

be to bite the hand that feeds it. And so, both here and in Ephesians, Paul warns the Gentiles to remember what they once were and what they are now, heirs and partakers of Israel's promises. In short, unless Gentile Christians remember the mystery of Christ and the mystery of the church, the predominately Gentile church will fall into the worst kind of religious pride, and even into the worst kind of anti-Semitism. Thinking itself to be something in its own right, thinking it has a direct line to God's election, the church will too readily look on the Jewish nation as cast off and the rest of the world as reprobate, all the while forgetting that it was once itself that world, without hope and without God, and that now it eats off Israel's table and lives off the fatness of that olive tree which is Israel.

Once again we are confronted here with the mystery of that elective and creative action of God which brings light out of darkness, life out of death, salvation out of unbelief. Out of Israel's unbelief God, in ways past our comprehension, fashions the election and salvation of the Gentiles. God bends and directs evil against itself, and out of its defeat brings forth that greatest good: salvation and unending life. As God creatively fashioned the redemption of mankind out of mankind's crucifixion of Jesus Christ, as he brings good out of evil, as he fashions the mystery of that new humanity which is the church out of the death of his Son, God fashions the salvation and election of the Gentiles out of the unbelief of Israel. To our knowledge the path of God's election and grace is indeed a riddle not unlike Samson's: "Out of the eater came something to eat. Out of the strong came something sweet" (Judg. 14:14).

Sixth, Paul declares, "Lest you be wise in your own conceits, I want you to understand this mystery, brethren." What is the mystery Paul is talking about? "A hardening has come upon part of Israel, until the full number of the Gentiles come in"—*in*, that is, to Israel's inheritance. When the full number of the Gentiles has come into Israel's election and all that goes with it, then "all Israel," corporate Israel, the *nation* will be saved.

As far as the gospel is concerned, unbelieving Israel is an enemy. But remember, says Paul to the Gentiles, "they are enemies of God *for your sake,"* and so far as election is concerned, Israel is beloved for their forefathers' sake, which is to say, because of God's election and promise to Abraham, Isaac, and Jacob. And this holds because the "gifts and the call of God are irrevocable." God's election of Israel is not something of which God repents. The Bible does speak of cases of divine repentance of an evil that God said he would do (for example, to Nineveh), but it speaks of no such repentance concerning God's election of Israel. On the contrary, it declares that God's calling of Israel and his gifts to them—the covenant, the promise, the Christ—are not subject to repentance and ultimate withdrawal.

If election and its gifts were subject to cancellation, the church could have no confidence in its own divine election or gifts. The church could not be assured that God would not abandon it because of its sin and unbelief. Recognition of this should keep Christians from being anti-church; conversely, failure to recognize this accounts for the considerable disdain and hostility that many Christians have toward the church and many churches toward the ecumenical movement. God has not cast off Israel because of its unbelief or even because of its rejection of Christ, but many Christians have cast off the church, and many denominations have washed their hands of *much* of the church for less reason. Furthermore, if God had cast off Israel because of her unfaithfulness, no individual believer could have any sure confidence that God might not cast him off because of his own sins and shortcomings.

Seventh, Paul sums up his position by telling the church at Rome that it was once disobedient to God but now has received mercy through the disobedience of Israel. But he also tells them this is not the final word. It is God's intent that *by* the mercy shown to the Gentiles, unbelieving Israel may also obtain mercy. This is the path God's elective grace takes in history. Since unbelieving Israel is an enemy of the gospel *for our sakes,* it will receive mercy through the mercy shown to us. For, Paul says in conclusion, God has consigned all men to disobedience so that he might, in this manner, have mercy upon all.

After threading his way along this zigzagging movement of

God's election in history, Paul breaks into a doxology that extols the depth and the richness of God's wisdom and knowledge, and declares that God's "ways are past finding out," and that, therefore, none could have advised him of the way his grace and election should take in history.

*   *   *

What we have said does not make everything transparently clear. But it does indicate without doubt that God's election of Israel holds in spite of Israel's unbelief, that the Gentiles through the church share in and partake of Israel's election, and that they do so that God's election of the nation of Israel may end in the salvation of this nation.

If the whole truth about biblical election were exhausted by the doctrine of individual election, Paul's cry of praise at the end of chapter 11 would be strange indeed. It is the complexity of the movements of God's elective action in history, which is unsearchable and inscrutable for our minds, that makes Paul's concluding doxology appropriate.

Within decretal theology, God's elective ways are so comprehensively searched out and scrutinized that the very necessity of election and grace is seen as grounded in the rational nature of God. It is true that some of the decretal theologians assert that finite minds can only have an analogical knowledge of God and his decree. Man is said to be incapable of knowing God's decree in the exhaustive manner in which God knows it. Man knows God's decree expansively, but not in the depth dimension of the divine. Nonetheless even this version of decretal theology is still capable of asserting confidently that God is the ultimate cause of sin and of reprobation—which quite well explains everything, if God is exhaustively rational as decretal theology maintains he is.

The Conclusion to the Canons of Dort asserts that God does not elect and reprobate in the same manner. Paul makes it clear in Romans that God does not elect Jews and Gentiles in the same manner. And it is equally clear that God does not elect Jesus Christ and the individual Christian in the same manner. But decretal theology cannot honor this rejection of the "in the same manner." It insists that the simple divine decree is without distinctions, though it appears to finite minds to have them. But if so, the Canons' insistence that God does not elect and reject "in the same manner" goes out the window. The rejection of the "in the same manner" causes decretal theology no end of trouble.

Election in biblical thought is never a selection, a taking of this and a rejection of that out of multiple realities. To be sure, God began Israel with Abram from Ur of the Chaldees; and Jesus was born out of Israel according to the flesh; and the church emerged out of Jew and Gentile. But God brought *life out of death.* None of these was what it became through election. Election is always a creative act. In biblical thought, Israel, Christ, and the church are not existing realities that God selectively chooses out of a number of extant Israels, Christs, or churches. Israel, Christ, and the church exist only because each is elected by God. They are created by the dynamics of election, for they are what they are only by virtue of their election.

The church would not be the church apart from its election. It might be a social club or a community of shared religious views, but it would not be the church. Because election is always in this sense exclusive and unique, there is only one Israel, one Christ, and one church. If there were more than one of each, God's election would in each case be arbitrary, and God's election is never arbitrary. What God elects he creates, and he does so for a purpose. Consequently, the election of each is a call to service, a summons to be a co-laborer with God in the actualization of God's elective purpose and goal. For this reason all forms of God's election are profoundly historical and eschatological. The election of Israel was not an end in itself. The election of Christ was not an end in itself—hence his servant form and service. And the election of the church is not an end in itself, for it must preach the gospel to all nations and every creature, making known to the principalities and powers of the heavenly places God's eternal purpose in Christ, and provoking unbelieving Israel to such jealousy as will arouse its passion to repossess its inheritance, its election, its Christ.

If Israel were a selection out of many nations, it would have a right to pride. Its election would be the ground of its pride. If Jesus had been a selection out of many existing Christs, his very selection would provide a basis for pride. If the church were selected out of many extant religious bodies, its selection itself would constitute a ground for pride. But no form of biblical election is a ground for pride, for each object of election owes its very *existence* to its election. And no nation, individual, or church has ground for pride if its very existence stems from its election.

CHAPTER IX

The Freedom of God
and the Logic of Election

The roots of decretal theology lie deep in the scholastic theological tradition. Scholasticism takes its name from the schools of the medieval period in which it developed. Then, as now, theologies that originated and developed in schools and not within the life of the church often had a deadening effect on the pulpit. Indeed, such theologies are frequently as little related to the pulpit as many of their creators are to the church. Many distinguished theologians rarely sit in the pew, and even less often occupy the pulpit.

Still, theologies born in the ivory towers of theologians who are anything but church fathers can have a fatal effect on the pulpit because preachers are so often awed by the theologians. The rationalistic tradition is so strong in the West that ministers feel obliged virtually to venerate the theologian because of the scientific and rational facilities he brings to bear on Christian truth, as though the calling of a theologian were higher than that of a minister. Ancient Israel had prophets, not theologians. Whatever theologizing Israel's prophets did they did as prophets speaking the prophetic word. The New Testament had apostles, and the theologizing they did occurred not in the remote, abstract realm of academia, but within their apostolic function of bearing witness to the resurrected Christ.

The most characteristic feature of medieval theological

scholasticism was its view that God and Christian truth are wholly definable in terms of rationality. This idea had its roots in Aristotle, for whom the Absolute (Aristotle's name for God) was exhaustively rational. God, for Aristotle, was *thought*. Not thought about a world, or thought about men; not thought about love, human or divine. Just thought, thinking about itself. Aristotle's God, therefore, is reason, all reason, and nothing but reason. What can such a God do? He can do nothing but contemplate himself. His only action is aesthetic: he directs his contemplation on the beauty and harmony of his own rationality.

For Aristotle, rationality could exist without personality. And so Aristotle's God was not a person, and since he was not personal, he had no will, no freedom, no freedom of will to decide to do anything other than rationally to reflect on what he exhaustively is, namely, thought.

At first the medieval scholastics had only translations of portions of Aristotle and the *Isagoge* of Porphyry to work with. This, however, sufficed to generate a problem that was one of the great preoccupations of the scholastics—the relationship of universals and particulars. The discussion was spirited and complex, but for the scholastic theologian the question at bottom concerned God's relationship to the world. How is God the great Universal related to all the particularities of our world? Later the scholastics came into possession of the whole of Aristotle's writings, obtaining them from the Jews of Spain, who had obtained them from the Arabs. With the recovery of these writings scholasticism— getting an assist from the neo-Platonic tradition of Augustine—burst into the theological ferment with which many of the great names of medieval theology are associated.

God continued to be regarded in terms of rationality. For Anselm all Christian truth is demonstrable. Aquinas did not agree, but he did contend that theology and philosophy are not at odds. (By philosophy Aquinas of course meant Greek philosophy as refined and corrected by Christian revelation.) Since both philosophy and theology come from God, they cannot be in contradiction. Aquinas conceived of God as the first cause of all things and the most real and perfect of all beings. Such considerations led him to a view of God's providence as all-comprehensive, and to his view of double predestination.

There were theologians who rejected the tendency to regard God as exhaustively rational, as the One whose essence is Being. Alongside the realist interpreters of universals arose the nominalists, who contended that reality resided more in the particulars than in the universals. Correspondingly, they urged that the essence of God was not being but will. The clue to God's nature did not lie in his rationality, nor in his essence understood as being, but in the divine will. The essence of God is volitional. For Duns Scotus God is absolute will. Whatever is right, is right simply because God willed it. Had God willed the opposite of what he in fact did will, what is now wrong would have been right, and right wrong. For William of Occam, Scotus' student, no theological truth is rationally demonstrable. One accepts the truth of Christianity only on the authority of the church. The church widely rejected this conception of God in terms of pure will, while it continued to theologize within the position of God as an exhaustively rational being—though not of course with anything like total unanimity and agreement among its theologians.

Sixteenth- and seventeenth-century Protestant scholasticism, which developed the decretal theology of the single decree, had its roots in this medieval scholasticism. Protestant scholasticism, too, tended to regard God as exhaustively rational, as the cause of all particular realities of created reality, and as having a universal all-comprehensive plan that determines whatever comes to pass.

This scholastic type of theology still persists in the Reformed theological community. It has come to the surface in the writings of theologians like Herman Hoeksema, Cornelius Van Til, Gordon Clark, and Lorraine Boettner. And it lies below the surface in the epistemologies of a host of contemporary evangelicals who are concerned about the nature of Scripture and revelation, and faith and history. Out of this concern a number of conflicting views about the nature of Christian apologetics have arisen.[1]

1 See *The Philosophy of Gordon H. Clark*, ed. Ronald H. Nash.

Although sharing the view that God is exhaustively rational, scholastic theologians do not always agree about the nature of human knowledge. Does a statement about God given in revelation or a statement about a fact of science or history mean the same for us as for God? In other words, do we know the truth about anything as exhaustively as God knows the truth about anything? Clark and Van Til are both decretal theologians, yet on this issue they sharply disagree. Clark holds that the meaning of any proposition is as exhaustively known to the human mind as to the divine mind. Since human rationality and logic are coextensive with divine rationality and logic, the truth of any revealed truth could be as fully known by man as by God. Because of this coincidence, Clark contends, the "Logos" of the prologue to the Fourth Gospel could be translated Logic. Logical coherence is a characteristic of truth, and the law of noncontradiction can be given full play. If a truth does not mean the same to us as it means to God we end up, Clark argues, in skepticism.

Van Til disagrees. Our knowledge, he says, is analogous to God's knowledge. We know in part, and so far forth we know truly. But our knowledge is never identical with God's knowledge of any truth. Van Til agrees that God is exhaustively rational and wholly logical, but because he alone is God and we are finite, the meaning of "the sky is blue," or "two plus two equals four," is not wholly identical for God and man. If it were, man would be equal to God in the area of knowledge. Since God alone is exhaustively rational, he alone knows any and all truths exhaustively. Finite man must be willing to accept his finitude, eschew human autonomy, and accept the fact that all truth appears to him as apparently contradictory. The idea that all truth appears to our finite minds as contradictory agrees with decretal theology's view of finite reality. The truth about reality is God's decree. The decree alone, urges Van Til, gives everything its meaning. But since the decree is simple, without distinguishable items, all finite reality appears to us as apparently contradictory, for we experience it only as a series of multiple, discrete, distinguishable items. But if history as we experience it is not real but only apparently real, reality itself is rendered suspect.

This threat to finite reality stems from decretal theology's identification of the decree with God's essence, not his will. The decree itself is seen as reality, and reality is not seen as something other than the decree—namely, that which is decreed. This identification of decree and reality is visible, as we have noted, in Hoeksema's definition of God's decree. "The counsel of God is the eternal reality of all things in God's conception." Here, all things are eternally real in God's decree of all things. What is historical reality, according to Hoeksema? The answer he gives in the remainder of his definition of God's decree is this: "the creatures (historical reality) are but the revelation [of the decree] in time and space."[2] Historical reality is "eternal," and in time and space it is *merely revealed*.

In this definition of reality in terms of the divine decree, it should be noted first that no distinctions are made—or can be made—between the realities of history, for example, between the creation, the Fall, and God's redemptive action in Christ. Second, neither creation nor redemption is true because it happened, for the truth of both is eternally real, and in time and space their eternal reality is simply *revealed*. Third, time and space, which are of the essence of the historical, are reduced to mere media of disclosure. Thus time and space, essential dimensions of history, fall *outside* the decree of decretal theology. They are not features of what God has decreed, and are no part of reality as constituted by the eternal decree. They are merely the *means* through which reality is disclosed.

This is clear indication that decretal theology cannot honor the historical. The historical has been excluded because the decree is defined in terms of God's necessary essence, not in terms of God's will or freedom. By defining the decree as it did, decretal theology failed to discover a transition from decree to history. Between the single, simple decree and the multiple realities of the created world and its history, lies decretal theology's "apparently contradictory." The distinctive feature of God's decree is said to be its simplicity, but this simplicity, it is said, can be known to finite minds only

2 *Reformed Dogmatics*, p. 155.

in terms of the opposite of simplicity, namely, distinguish-able moments and discrete parts. This means that God's decree is for us wholly unknowable. Time and space render it unknowable, for time and space are not an ingredient of the decree, but merely the media in which its eternal reality is revealed.

If no knowledge of God's decree is possible, since all our knowledge of what it decrees lacks the simplicity that is the distinctive feature of the decree and is indeed marked by the apparently contradictory, we do end in skepticism, as Clark warned. Yet the solution is not to identify the nature of human knowledge with divine knowledge. For the origin of the loss of real human knowledge is decretal theology's construing of the decree in such a way as to exclude any real transition from God to world, with the result that, in terms of the decree, there is nothing to know.

Herman Dooyeweerd has criticized Van Til's view that God is exhaustively rational on the ground that it leads him to overlook the distinction between "truths of reason" and "truths of fact." This failure, says Dooyeweerd, "would make even the central facts of creation, fall into sin, and redemption a consequence of logical necessity" and "would result in an extreme logistic view of 'God's world plan' which would leave no room for the sovereign freedom of God's will. For God's will can, in your view, only *carry out* the plan of God, not *determine* it."[3] One might add that (as the nature of decretal theology itself indicates) a divine will that cannot *determine* the decree also cannot *execute* the decree. The ability to do the one is the ability to do the other. It is precisely the inability of God's will in decretal theology to *execute* the decree that accounts for the contradiction (real, not apparent) between the nature of the decree and the nature of creation and history. And Van Til cannot resolve this contradiction except by asserting that one must in faith declare it to be only apparent.

Loyal to the scholastic rationalist tradition, Van Til holds that God is exhaustively rational. He is therefore obliged to make God's will an unfree agent of divine rationality. God's

3 *Jerusalem and Athens*, pp. 88f.

will can execute his decree, but is not free to determine it. With this we are at the heart of Turretin and decretal theology's single decree.

*   *   *

This brief discussion of the scholastic understanding of God's rationality has been given as background for the suggestions this chapter will make about understanding God's decree in terms of his freedom. Turretin's theology of the divine decree is a classic example of Reformed scholasticism. Since we have already given some attention to Turretin's view of God's decree, we can now present his basic view briefly.

Turretin believed that God was exhaustively rational. On this point he stood in the tradition of Aristotle and Greek philosophy. Since Turretin was a Christian theologian, however, he believed (as Aristotle did not) that God was a personal and volitional being, that is, a being with a will, who could make a decree. Our interest is to see how Turretin understood God as an exhaustively rational being *and* as a volitional being. Did Turretin bring a baptized and corrected Aristotelianism into Christian theology that could make a contribution to a proper understanding of God and his decree? Or did Aristotelianism dominate Turretin's understanding of how God's rationality and God's freedom are related? Having endorsed the basic Aristotelian understanding of God as an exhaustively rational being, was Turretin able, within this commitment, to do justice to the freedom of God's decree? The answer is No. The very Christian features of God in terms of which Aristotle was to be corrected, his personality and his freedom, suffered under the heavy preponderance of Aristotle's notion of an exhaustively rational God. Turretin held that God's decree is identical with his essence. As far as God's will is concerned, the decree was simply God's essence in its act of willing what shall exist outside of God. "In this sense the decrees are rightly said to be identical with his own essence." As far as God's rational essence is concerned, the decree "is nothing other than the divine essence itself, as it is known by God."[4]

4 Locus IV, Question 1, vii, viii.

Thus the decree is the volitional implication of the divine essence. God's will is so identified with his essence that the former is not free to will anything but that which the latter demands. The decree, therefore, both as fact and content, is as absolutely necessary as the divine essence is necessary. God could not be without a decree, and the decree could not be other than it is. Turretin answers his own question about how the decree exists in God by asserting that the decree exists "essentially" and not "accidentally" in God. An "accidental" decree would possess the dimensions of the unnecessary, the contingent, the historical, the novel. If the decree derived from the freedom of the divine will, the decree would exist in God as an accident. Such a decree, urges Turretin, would violate God's simplicity and perfection, for it would represent an "addition" to God. And it would violate God's immutability, "since the accidental is the root of all change."[5]

But if God's decree exists in him essentially because it is the volitional implication of his essence, what of the freedom of God? If God's will can will only what his essence demands, can we indeed speak of God's freedom? Turretin does speak of God's freedom, but he defines it within the determination of the divine will in terms of the divine essence. On this view God's freedom is very peculiar and limited. God is said to be free only in the sense that he cannot be affected or conditioned by anything outside himself. If this meant to say no more than that nothing finite can push the infinite into a corner, that no sinner could manipulate God into being gracious, no one would object. But for Turretin God's freedom from the world includes the idea that God himself is not free, if he wills, to respond to and accommodate his actions to what is external to him. God's grace, for example, cannot be regarded as God's free response to human sin. This understanding of God's freedom explains why (as we shall see later) Paul's teaching about God's eternal purpose in Christ plays no role in a decretal formulation of God's decree, for Paul describes that purpose as a response to the sinful brokenness of human existence. On Turretin's view, on the other

5 Locus IV, Question 1, xiii.

hand, God bears the marks of Aristotle's Unmoved Mover. He
is regarded as the cause of whatever lies outside of himself,
and necessarily so, but he is not free to respond freely in
grace to a sinful world; he is not free to respond in Christ
with a purpose that is essentially gracious.

How pervasively this view has penetrated and shaped Reformed theology! Here is the theological bottomland from
which has arisen what is often regarded as the correct Reformed understanding of God's immutability and of sovereignty. Here is the source of the assertion that God is the
cause and source of sin, yet not responsible for it. Here is the
root of an unconditional theology that not only rightly
rejects Arminian theology (although with wrongly formulated reasons) but which also insists that God is so imper-
turbable that he is not free to be moved with compassion for
the plight of man. Here is the origin of the position that
reprobation is ultimately not an act of divine justice *in
response* to sin, but something that has its ground in God
himself. Here arise Reformed theology's tendency to ignore
history and eschatology and decretal theology's tendency to
cast a threatening shadow over all reality. For if the decree is
indeed identical with God's essence, the essence of what God
decrees *is his own essence.* Such a decree—and such a decreeing God—cannot get outside of itself. The decree, like God's
essence, bears no relation to the world. Between the two is a
wide chasm, which God, as understood by decretal theologians, cannot cross, and which, moreover, he need not cross;
for if the essence of what God decrees is his own essence,
there really is no gap between God's essence and what God
wills, for there is no world outside of God.

*   *   *

This gap between God and world, between decree and
reality, is only crossed by God's freedom. But this freedom
must be rightly understood. The freedom of Turretin and of
decretal theology is negative—God cannot be affected by, nor
respond to, anything external to him. As regards the will of
God as it relates to his decree, Turretin urges that it is not
free. The decree is not accidental, for God could not exist

without it. The decree *is* God, the essence of God in its volitional activity. Such a will is not free; it can only will what is God. It is not free to will what is not-God, a world; it is not free to *do* what is not-God, that is, to enter the world and become personally involved in it.

Moreover, since God is regarded as exhaustively rational, if the divine will should will anything other than God's essence, if it should will some other reality than the reality of God, then what it willed would be irrational. Obviously, the strand of scholasticism in the theologies of many Reformed thinkers has not gone at this point beyond the rationalism inherited from Aristotle. The reinterpretation of Aristotle that intended to make room for the Christian idea of God as personal and possessed of will, failed. Once God is defined as *exhaustively* rational, no room is left for his will and freedom. Turretin reduces God's will to an activity of the divine essence. The same thing happens to God as personal. An exhaustively rational God is necessarily an exceedingly impersonal God, neither personally in, nor affected by, anything or anybody in the world.

God is rational, not irrational. But this is not to say that he is *exhaustively* rational, for to say that would mean that rationality exhaustively defines him, that he is so completely of the nature of rationality as to be wholly interpretable in terms of reason. As we have seen, however, decretal scholastic theologians do not hold that God is thus exhaustively interpretable to our finite rationality. Such knowledge as God has given man in his revelation is valid, but it is not exhaustive, for man's finite mind cannot fathom the heights and depths of God, of his decree, of Christian truth. We know in part. We see in a mirror darkly. The scholastic strand of Reformed theology holds that while he does not appear thus to our minds, God is in fact exhaustively rational.

Decretal theologians claim to get this conception of God from the Bible. But nowhere in Scripture does it say that God is wholly and exhaustively rational. The scholastic equation of God with rationality owes more to the rationalistic philosophical tradition than to Scripture. When Turretin reduces the will of God to the activity of God's essence and

identifies the decree with the essence of God, he is bringing
strange fires to the altar.

God's will is no less definitive of God than is his essence,
and is no less free than his essence is necessary. This is no
novel assertion: it is as old as the history of Christian
thought. Where this is granted, God is seen as free, not indeed
to contradict his essence, but to do whatever accords with—
but is not demanded by—it. God is free to create what is
not-God. The world is such a creation. Such a creation does
not contradict the essence or nature of God, but it is, by all
the norms of Christian orthodoxy, something that God's
essence did not *require*. The divine will to create is something
other than Turretin's volitional action of the divine essence.
In other words, God's creation of the world as his free act is
not contrary to his rationality, but something other than his
rationality *requires*. This is God's positive, internal freedom.
Creation is the cross that every rationalism must bear. Rationalism seeks to reduce everything to itself, but between a
necessary God and a contingent creation lies a gap that
rationalism cannot bridge. For there stands God's free act of
creation, a freedom that rationality—even in its absolute form
as rationalism—cannot absorb into its own inherent necessity.

Similarly, the freedom of God means that God's decree is
also an act of divine freedom. God is free to exist without a
decree as well as without a world. Rationalism tends to make
everything necessary. For Hoeksema, it makes reprobation
necessary for election. For Van Til, necessity determines that
common grace ripens men for the day of judgment. For
Turretin, the cross must be, for "those reprobates who ar-
ranged for Christ's crucifixion . . . , the means of damnation,
and that it was so depended on the most just decree of God."

A similar necessity is said to govern God's decree. The
decree, according to Turretin, is the "vital" action of God's
essence. It possesses the highest possible necessity, for it is
identical with God's essence. It is ontologically eternal in the
same sense in which God is ontologically eternal. (How,
indeed, could it be otherwise, if it is identical to God's
essence and its content the volitional activity of God's essence?) Such a decree, as Turretin was at some pains to urge
and demonstrate, is one of necessity, not of divine freedom.

The authentic, biblical view of God's freedom would seem to be that God is free, both in terms of his essence and of his will, to have a decree and create a world, or not. Either alternative would accord with his nature. On such a view, God's will is not merely free to carry out the decree (which is the only freedom Turretin thinks the divine will has), but also to determine it.

It is no accident that in scholastic Reformed theology God's sovereignty has increasingly been dissociated from his grace and associated instead with his determination of all things. Similarly, election has been dissociated from soteriology (where it is in Calvin) and associated instead with a general doctrine of divine predestination. When everything is regarded as essentially and exhaustively rational, nothing is distinguishable from anything else. In the darkness of rationalism everything is a cow and all cows are black. In the pulpit, to lecture on predestination and to preach on election turn out to be the same thing, and in fact the church no longer hears about that freedom of God which is the clue to the secret of grace and election. The wonder and the mystery are gone, and election is a topic for debates. Aristotle said that philosophy started when man began to wonder. But when philosophical rationalism has done its work, the wonder evaporates from Christianity and the mystery departs. If God and his decree, and in consequence, the world and its history no less, are exhaustively rational, the gospel need not be preached, for there would be nothing for preaching to accomplish, since everything would remain rational whether men respond in faith or unbelief. Even rejection of the gospel is part and parcel of its rationality.

The freedom of God, then, is the freedom of the divine will, not to carry out the alleged volitions of the divine essence, not to will a mere replica of the divine essence, but to will something other than the divine essence, something that is not-God, something that is, as regards God, other, real, novel. Such a conception of divine freedom allows for the full reality of what God decrees to create, and for the reality of a world not threatened by a decree in which what God decrees is his own essence.

Turretin contended that if God's decree were accidental—

not identical with his essence—it would be an addition to God. But the freedom of God means precisely that it can be the source of that which is not-God. God's freedom is a source out of which a resolve can arise, as God wills, to create a world. But this *resolve* to create a world is no more *God* than is the act of creating the world. God's acts are surely *God's,* but they are not themselves *God.* The ontological confusion that regards as strictly divine a resolve of the divine will is a fountain of profound error. If a resolve of the divine will is ontologically identical with God, then there is no reason for not saying about God's act of creation (and, indeed, about all his acts in history) that it is identical with God. From there it is but a short step to declaring that all reality is divine.

Turretin would doubtless respond that the resolve of the divine will is different because it occurs *in* God. But the fact that the resolve is an act of his freedom, not of his essence, indicates that it is not in the ontological sense God. And precisely because it is such an act of the divine freedom, it is, from the perspective of God's necessary essence, an additional something, a change, something new.

The fact that something occurs in God does not necessarily mean that the occurrence is divine. Paul says our lives are hid with Christ in God (Col. 3:3), but that does not make our lives divine. Our election is an internal act of God, but it is not on that account *divine,* in the ontological sense (though we speak of divine election to characterize it as *God's* act). If Turretin were right to insist that the decree is ontologically identical with God, and is thus in the strictest sense divine, our election would be divine in the same sense. This would mean that God needs the elect, and since a perfect being has what it needs, the elect themselves would be divine.

Turretin's difficulty is really a problem of "in" and "out." He has an "in-theology" that cannot become an "out-theology." Because he holds that whatever occurs *in* God *is* God, Turretin sees God as unable to get out to that which is not-God, that is, to an *act* of creation and into creation itself. This in-theology has no exit because of its identification of decree with divine essence. This equation of decree with essence leads Turretin to regard God's decree as eternal and simple in the same sense in which God is eternal and simple. This leads decretal theology into a morass from which there is no extrication.

A decree whose eternality is identical with God's eternality lacks a point or moment of transition. And there can be no point of transition unless God, in his freedom, freely wills to make a decree and to effectuate it in the space-time world. A decree that is identical with God's eternal, necessary, and unchanging essence cannot move out of itself. If God's essence were a point of transition, he would necessarily go out of himself, create a world, and redeem it; but then everything would be necessary.

Moreover, if God's decree is marked by the same simplicity that marks the being of God, it is indeed a simple decree, without parts, moments, or distinctions, and its realization is also without parts, moments, or distinction. In other words, both the world and its history are a simple, indistinguishable mass, and our empirical experience of successive moments, discrete items, distinguishable parts and elements is unreal. As the theologians of the single decree insist, our experience is merely the way things appear to our historically conditioned minds. If this is true about our experience, not only are time and history apparitions, but there is no distinction between God as the cause of good and God as the cause of sin, between election and reprobation, between election and a generalized predestination.

The same consequences follow if the strictly divine simplicity of the decree is urged, as Berkhof does, in terms of God's knowledge. The decree is simple as God is simple, because God knows its content immediately, instantaneously, all-at-once. If God knows his decree in this fashion, Berkhof argues, it must be a distinctionless decree. If so, the world of space and time and all the varieties of nature and history as a single datum must be a reality without predicates, a temporality without moments, a space without measurement or content, a mass without distinguishable features.

The freedom of God means that God is free, if he wills, to have a decree other than himself, and therefore neither eternal nor simple in the sense in which he is both eternal and simple.

This does not mean that God's decree is not eternal: the Scriptures teach clearly enough that it is. But its eternality does not stem from God's necessary eternality—if it did, it would be pantheistically identical with God. Its eternality stems rather from God's eternal exercise of his freedom to have a decree and to actualize it.

The proper view of the eternality of God's decree is similar to the view Origen mistakenly applied to the generation of the second person of the trinity. Origen believed that the Son is eternally generated by the Father, but he diverged from classical orthodoxy by asserting that the Father's generation of the Son was not a necessity of God's essence but an act of his volition. This view the church rightly declared heretical, because it was applied to what is divine, the second person of the trinity. But what Origen said is the truth when applied to what is not divine, namely, God's decree. Conversely, the orthodox view of the eternality of the Son is heresy when applied to the decree. For the decree, unlike the Son, is not divine. The decree is an "addition"; the Son is not.

The freedom of God means that God is eternally free to will to have a decree and to move out of himself into space and time to actualize what he decreed. The expression that God is free to move out of himself must not be understood as though God moved into *something*, perhaps time and space. Time and space are not independent entities into which God could move. They are not an envelope, as the ancient pagan philosophies thought, in which life is lived and history occurs. Some Christian theologians reflect a pagan perspective on time and space by regarding existence as unqualified by grace and, as regards the purpose of God, as a neutral continuum. Indeed, all decretal theologians tend to regard time and space as merely media within which God actualizes his decree.

Time and space are essential for the historical. But if God's decree were eternal in the absolute divine sense in which God is eternal, time and space could only be reduced to a theater in which the decree is revealed. In such a view time and space would not belong to the essence of what is revealed. Time and space could only be regarded as defective and faulty finite media that distort the divine decree by breaking up its simplicity and singularity and refracting it as multiple. History is then something that by its very character distorts the single decree.

But this is too Kantian an understanding of space and time. In Christian thought space and time are not mere media through which God comes to actualize his decree and disclose his revelation. Space and time, as aspects of the historical, are of the essence of the message revealed. Space and time are ingredients of the decree, expressions of the fact that God in his freedom moves out of himself—out of his eternality—to create man and to be with and for man. Thus space and time are not so much signs of our finitude as signs of God's freedom. Indeed, space and time are the outward expression of the truth that God, in his freedom to decree, decided eternally, within himself, to have time and space for man, to have what Turretin called an "addition" and rejected as untrue and unacceptable.

The freedom of God, therefore, means that God is free to will, as he in fact did from all eternity, his resolve to create man and his world, to be involved with man and his world even to the point of becoming man in order in this profound and amazing way to be for and with man.

If the decree of God stems from the freedom of his will, not from the necessity of his essence, his decree is in its very nature of the character of the temporal, the historical, the new. Turretin rightly perceived that if God's decree is necessary because grounded in the necessity of his essence, it is not an "addition," something new, something that bespeaks change, something historical. Thus grounding God's decree, Turretin had to exclude all such additions, since none of them could properly be predicated of God's essence. But if God's decree stems from an exercise of his freedom, it is not of the nature of his eternality and simplicity but of the nature of the historical, with all the multiplicity of temporality, parts, discrete items, and distinguishable moments.

If our empirical experience of the historical is real (and not merely apparent on account of our finite vision), God willed the historical with its very real moments and distinguishable parts. And if that is so, historicity is a characteristic of God's decree. There is a history that precedes our history. It is the history of God's freedom, in which God engaged in an unnecessary, yet eternal action neither demanded by his essence, nor ontologically identifiable with him. There is *in* God a history that has its origin and content in the freedom of God's will, a history that is not-God, even though it occurred in God. The possibility of this lies in God's freedom; its actuality stems from God's exercise of this freedom.

Rationalism has tried to reduce Christianity to its own terms and to the limits of its own possibilities. When rationalism functions in Christian theology it is sometimes difficult to see what is being done. It is easier to make a critical analysis of, say, Hegel than of a decretal theologian like Turretin. But Turretin's decretal theology is subject to a much more simple evaluation. It can be judged by a simple appeal to matters on which all Christians are agreed.

According to Turretin, God's decree and all that it contains (and it contains everything) is necessary.[6] If so, it was *absolutely necessary* for God to be gracious to you and me as Christians. His essence demanded it. Similarly, God was obliged by his own nature to forgive your sins, to elect you, to send Christ to die for you. If as a Christian you know God's grace as his freely willed, unnecessary goodness toward you, you know that on this matter of God's decree Turretin is wrong. Or again, if as a Christian you do not believe that any man can be eternally reprobated to hell just because God's essence had to will his damnation, you know that Turretin's doctrine of God's decree is wrong. In simple terms, if God is exhaustively rational and his decree identical with his essence, the decree is not only absolutely necessary and wholly rational, but God's election of every man is also

6 In Locus IV, Question 2, xiii, Turretin seems to go back on his identification of God's will with his essence. He says that if God had wished he could have refrained from making all things, and contrasts this with the "necessary connection" between Father and Son. But if we read this carefully, Turretin appears to be saying only that nothing imposes a limitation on the freedom of God as does the Son, in the sense in which the Father is not free to be without the Son. That is, God's *essence* is free as regards all creative things in a sense in which God's essence is not free as regards the Son. This freedom of God, therefore, is a freedom of God's essence, not the freedom of God's will. God's freedom, of course, is not wholly unrelated to his essence, God cannot will what is against his essence. But he can and does will what his essence does not demand.

necessary and wholly reasonable. What Christian would dare say this about his own election?

If God *must* love me because he is God, his love for me would lose its meaning. But if God loves me freely, I can find no language that can do any better than stammer my love and praise and adoration of him. Any doxology I can raise is broken and faulty. Rationalism cannot understand such halting and unspoken worship. According to rationalism, everything is open and transparent. Rather than worship, it contemplates an aesthetic God who in turn does nothing more than aesthetically contemplate his own beauty and harmony.

If all this is true, a different light is cast on God's determination of whatever comes to pass. In decretal theology this determination means that whatever happens is *ipso facto* what God wills. No purpose runs through the stream of events. God is not progressively achieving his purpose through what happens. Each event is itself God's will and without qualification what God purposed. This static view of history flows directly from the scholastic tenet that God's decree is identical with his essence. Such a decree cannot be historical.

Paul's assertion that God "accomplishes all things according to the counsel of his will" (Eph. 1:12) is statically reinterpreted by decretal theology to mean that God determines whatever comes to pass. God's accomplishment is not an action in history, but a determination from above history that determines every event. But the very context in which Paul makes this assertion is a discussion of God's making known to us the mystery of his will, "according to his purpose which he set forth in Christ as a plan for the fulness of time, to unite all things in him, things in heaven and the things on earth" (1:9,10). God's will and purpose are in no sense equated with whatever comes to pass, but with his action achieved in and through Christ to unite all things in the Son. When this uniting is finally accomplished, the mystery of God's will shall be fully disclosed and God's eternal purpose *in* Christ will be realized in and through Christ. God works in and through and on all things to bend them to the realization of this eternal purpose. Paul reminds the Ephesians of what God has done in Christ, and of what God will yet do through Christ. Paul does not direct their eyes and fix their hope on whatever comes to pass, but on what is coming to pass through all things, namely, the divine positioning of Jesus, who will subject all things to himself. God is realizing, not the decretal resolve of his essence, but the free resolve of his will in the exercise of its freedom. When Paul declares to the Romans that all things work together for good to those who love God, he is *not* saying that whatever comes to pass is good, but that God sovereignly and graciously works on all things to make all things serve the good of those who love God.

Decretal theology asserts that God wills everything and that everything is, therefore, rational. Biblical thought, by contrast, sees many things as contrary to God's will and therefore irrational. In biblical thought what God does not will he can employ against itself and cause to work for good. God does not will sin or death. Yet God can use, work upon, bend, and overrule death for his saving purpose. God uses death to overcome death. God's sovereignty and the nature and purpose of his decree are not disclosed in a divine determination of whatever comes to pass, but in his sovereign freedom to overcome and destroy death *by death,* as he did through Jesus' death, and thus use sin and death to accomplish, *against* their nature, what he in his freedom decreed.

*   *   *

The distinctive feature of God's decree is that it expresses the freedom of the divine will. God is free not only to be as he is in himself, but also, if he wills, to move out of himself, to will and to create that which is not-God. God is free to create a world of time and space, free to create a man in his own image, and free to have time for man. Though he was not lonely, God freely willed not to be alone. He in freedom wanted a finite neighborhood around him, a created world and man alongside his own reality.

God's creation of the world is an act of divine self-giving, for the universe reveals something of the power and wisdom and goodness of God. Creation is a form of divine revelation. God in freedom created the world so that man might exist and know and love and live with God in God's blessedness. In an act of freedom God opens up the secret of his being and enables man to share in God's own life, power, glory, freedom, and joy. God's connection with the world is profoundly different from the mere external relationship posited by decretal theology. God's relation to the world is one of self-giving and self-communication. How else would the universe be revelatory of God?

If we regard it from the point of view of the reality of God, the creation of the world is an amazing decision. God is God alone. Beside him there is none else. He necessarily exists. He needs nothing. The creation of finite, contingent, unnecessary reality, then, in order that man, who is not God, might share in, know, love, and live with God, staggers the human mind. The truth of creation evades man's every rational attempt to comprehend. Philosophy may try to eliminate our sense of wonder at this; science may do the same by dissolving all the mystery of the universe. But true religion begins with wonder and never loses it. For creation is the wonder of God, the new and novel surprise of his freedom to extend and share his love—that is, to share himself.

But God's freedom has even greater heights and depths. For nowhere is God's freedom more fully expressed than in his resolve to become himself historical, a man existing in space and time in Jesus Christ, and in his Son to become involved in a world of sin and death, and through death to conquer and eliminate sin and death. God is so free that he can, in order to achieve the intention that man know him, love him, and live with him in eternal blessedness, deliver his own Son to the power of sin and death. God is so free that he can elect his own Son for the cross so that, in spite of all man's sin and evil, man may still share God's eternal life, beauty, glory, and joy.

Greater freedom cannot be imagined. What God elected Jesus to be the Christ for, and what God in his amazing freedom accomplished in him, falls far beyond the furthest reach of human reason. The more the human mind reflects on what God did in his freedom at Calvary, the greater the wonder becomes, and the more rational reflection gives way to joy and worship. The ineffable wonder of it arises out of the freedom of God, the freedom in which God is free to bear forever the name of Abraham, Isaac, and Jacob, and to make that name his memorial for all generations; the freedom that allows men to bear God's name and be known as his people. All this is free grace, stemming from the freedom of God, who is so free that he can impart himself to what is not-God.

Seen thus, this divine decree carries along a summons to the church to share with all men the long-hidden mystery of Christ, God's eternal purpose in him, and the gracious character of the divine decree. It is a call to make known the mystery of Israel's election and creation, the mystery of the church's election and creation, the mystery disclosed in God's election and creation of Jesus Christ. And this mystery of Christ is to be made known both by the church's proclamation of the Christ, and by the concrete life of the church in conformity to the nature and purpose of her existence and conduct. When the church preaches and lives that way, she is truly disclosing the eternal elective purpose of God in Christ.

*   *   *

Protestant scholasticism—like the medieval variety—was the end-product of an attempt to blend Aristotle and Christianity. The Aristotelianism was purified somewhat: for Aristotle's impersonal Absolute a personal creator God was substituted. But Aristotle's rationalism, according to which God was defined as exhaustively rational, was retained. This was combined with a divine decree that defined God's relationship to the world in terms of a modification of Aristotle's notion of causality. It was generally conceded that all things are completely transparent only to the mind of God. Finite man could only attain to a kind of the knowledge God possesses through such routes as mysticism, negation (the *via negationis*), affirmation (the *via eminentia*), or analogy.

Speaking out of a scholastic tradition, with a decree wholly definable in terms of rationality, Reformed theologians have often contended that election and reprobation are closely related; indeed, they have urged that election logically implies reprobation. Lorraine Boettner says that if election is true, "reprobation will follow of logical necessity."[7] Berkhof urged that "reprobation naturally follows from the logic of the situation. The decree of election naturally implies the decree of reprobation. ... If He has chosen some, then He has by that very fact also rejected others."[8] And Abraham Kuyper, though he admitted that reprobation is not explicitly taught in Scripture, urged that it lies in the very structure of biblical truth.[9]

Given the character of the decree as they see it, decretal theologians have sufficient reason for positing a logical nexus between election and reprobation. This logical nexus, however, requires that God elects and reprobates "in the same manner." If the decree is a logical harmony, everything in it is logically and rationally interrelated in the same manner. Exhaustively rational relationships allow no distinctions. Election then implies reprobation as logically as reprobation implies election. But such a view violates the "in the same manner" rejected by the Canons of Dort and leaves no room for the freedom of God. Election and reprobation both become necessary, and with this necessity theology loses all need for the language of grace. Indeed, we have noted earlier that the concept of grace is distorted in the thought of the thorough-going decretal theologian.

The basic objection to relating election and reprobation in such a way that the very fact of election posits reprobation lies in the freedom of God. If election is an act of divine freedom, there is nothing in its nature that necessarily posits reprobation, and to draw such deductions from it imposes on the nature of grace. No Christian acting in faith draws extrabiblical inferences from the nature of his election and projects them as rational necessities to which God is bound. For all the certain and assured nature of God's promises in Christ, the voice of faith does not tell the Almighty that he is

7 *The Reformed Doctrine of Predestination*, p. 123. "The very terms 'elect' and 'election' imply the terms 'non-elect' and 'reprobation.' When some are chosen out others are left not chosen" (p. 104). But the "some" is not contained in the *very term* "elect." Number has nothing to do with the *nature* of election. If God had chosen all men in Christ, only the *number* of the chosen would change, not the nature of election.

8 Cf. *Systematic Theology*, pp. 117f.

9 *Dictaten Dogmatiek*, I, vii, 252.

absolutely obligated to do this or that. The voice of faith uses the language of grace, which is the language of prayer.

In their rational understanding of election and reprobation, decretal theologians infer reprobation not so much from the nature of election as from the nature of number. From the proposition that "some men are elected" they deduce that "some are not." The ideas of number and limitation are attached to election. If a limited number of men are elect, it is assumed to follow that the remaining number must be rejected. But it is theologically perilous to define election in terms of number and limitation. Out of this matrix soon comes the definition of other Christian doctrines in terms of limitation, for example, the atonement. But if limited atonement, why not a limited death, a limited resurrection, a limited Christ? Why stop anywhere?

If the view developed in these pages is correct, if God's one decree is Christ and the heart of the decree is an election that in its unity embraces Christ and in terms of him Israel and the church, the idea of number as definitive of election is improper and unnecessary. For a view of election defined by number is an individualistic one. It finds the universalistic language of Scripture indigestible. For that reason such a view has never been developed into a doctrine of election that takes the profound biblical thought about Jews and Gentiles seriously.

The logic of election as it appears in Scripture is something quite different. The election of Israel does not imply the reprobation of all other nations. On the contrary, Israel's unique and exclusive election was a declaration that she—and God through her—would be a blessing to *all* nations. This election was fulfilled in Jesus Christ, and this election accounts both for the existence of the church and the peculiar function of the church to preach the gospel to all nations. The logic of the biblical view of election is a logic of freedom and grace and outward looking. Its movement is not exclusive but inclusive, as the development of election through Israel and Christ to the existence and growth of the worldwide church demonstrates.

If the logic of election were reprobation, and if the essence of election lay in individuality, the election of *one* nation (the Jews) would entail the rejection of all other nations. Moreover, the combination of logic and individualism would provide a basis from which an elect individual could argue that *all* others are reprobate. Although this sounds extreme, it is clear from church history that religious communities deeply committed to a doctrine of individual election often demonstrate precisely this religious psychology: they tend to consider all other individuals and churches to be rejected by God.

In one sense it is profoundly true that the full reality of election lies in one single elect person—namely, Jesus as the Elect of God. Jesus as the Christ is God's Elect as is no other man or nation. He is uniquely God's chosen, and is thus the ground and meaning of the election of Israel and of the election of the church. Jesus is God's Elect *par excellence;* therefore, any individual who projects himself as God's elect apart from Jesus' election projects himself as a "false elect."

But Jesus, of course, is not God's elect apart from his brethren. Paul says that those whom God foreknew "he also predestined to be conformed to the image of his Son, in order that he [Jesus] might be the first-born among many brethren" (Rom. 8:29). Without his brethren, Jesus would not be *first*-born. This is the point at which individual election must be defined—in the one individual who embodies the fulness of election. Reformed theology, however (and other theological traditions as well), has developed only a doctrine of *individual* election, a doctrine informed by the mathematical idea of limitation, the election of one. And in that doctrine, the one is not Jesus; the one of individual election is rather every elect person. Because this doctrine was developed without reference to the supreme model of individual election, it bears no internal relation to the election of Jesus.

The consequences of individualizing the doctrine of election are serious. For there is nothing in such a doctrine that relates elect to elect. The notion of the church as the *body* of Christ, a body in which Christians are members of each other, was diminished to an idea of a number of people rather than a community of the elect. This mathematical understanding of the church impoverishes the biblical understanding of the church as corporate, societal, and communal. It also provided a theological opening for the emergence and growth of the

wholly individualistic free church motif that denies the covenant, rejects infant baptism, and attacks ecumenism. Such a
notion shapes a large sector of the church, especially in the
United States.

When one's doctrine of election does not consider anyone
else's election (and indeed dwells on the likelihood of the
reprobation of others), election has become an exclusive
rather than an inclusive doctrine. It generates gloom not
praise, antithesis and judgment, not hope and mission. It
tends to kill the missionary impulse. It fosters the profoundly
un-Christian attitude that everyone is to be thought reprobate until he demonstrates the opposite. In short, it leads
Gentile Christians to forget what Paul told them to remember, that they themselves were once aliens and outsiders, not
heirs of but strangers to the covenant promises of God,
indeed, people without God and hope in the world.

CHAPTER X

Election and Preaching

Can election be preached? If the question refers to the election of Jesus, the answer is clearly affirmative. New Testament preaching is marked by its proclamation of God's election of Jesus as the Christ. There is no inherent difficulty in preaching the election of Jesus. Again, if the question refers to the election of Israel or of the church, the answer must again be yes. There is no inherent difficulty in preaching the election of Israel or of the church.

But can *individual* election be preached? Now the problem is a bit more difficult. We saw earlier how theologians have struggled with "the election of some men" and "a gospel that must be preached to all men," and how certain Scottish theologians limited the preaching of the gospel to those whose election could be antecedently established. The Canons of Dort reflect something of this same difficulty in their caution that individual election must be preached "in due time and place." The appropriate place is the church of God, but the "due time" is not further defined. The Canons seem to suggest that election be preached after a person has become a Christian, not, in other words, as part of missionary proclamation.

Dort's word of caution, not unlike the position of the seventeenth-century Scottish theologians we mentioned, seems to imply that election can only be preached to the elect, and thus is a truth that *explains* why a person is a Christian. The preaching of election is more the proclamation of something that accounts for a man's Christian existence than of something in which man is summoned to believe by the gospel. This explanatory function is an imposition placed on the doctrine of election by the rational, explanatory function that decretal theology accords the divine predestinating decree. In a decree whose distinctive feature is that it accounts for whatever happens, election is a principle of explanation rather than the good news. Naturally, that kind of doctrine of individual election does not form the content of the church's proclamation. Insofar as election is regarded as explanation, it ceases to be proclamation. Authentic preaching, on the other hand, is exposition of the Word, not an explanation of it.[1]

It is important to recognize that these difficulties characterize only the doctrine of individual election. No other doctrine of the Christian faith, rightly defined, is encumbered with these problems. No other doctrine that the gospel summons men to believe lingers in the background as an explanation of why men believe instead of something belonging to the faith. Individual election is the only doctrine that the church cannot freely call men to accept in faith, the only doctrine the church can preach only to the elect, the only doctrine that it must, with caution, preach only "in due time and place."[2]

*   *   *

We said that no inherent difficulty attaches to the church's proclamation that God elected *one* nation, *one* Jesus who is the only Christ, and *one* church. Only individual election poses special difficulties for proclamation and Christian faith.

---

[1] When election is regarded strictly as explanation, the same fate befalls it as befell common grace, limited atonement, and reprobation. As *explanations,* they are unpreachable.

[2] Canons of Dort, I, 15. The Westminster Confession speaks of the "high mystery of predestination" and urges that it "be handled with special prudence and care" (III,8). Why it is a high mystery that calls for special handling is not indicated. Yet it is clear that behind these assertions of both Dort and Westminster lies the dark possibility of nonelection, the kind of secret and mystery that adheres to no other Christian doctrine.

From what does this peculiar character of individual election stem?

First, it stems from the consideration that the doctrine of individual election was forged within a conception of a divine decree that is neither fully revealed in Jesus Christ nor fully known to faith in Jesus Christ, because it is regarded as an occurrence outside of Jesus Christ. On this view, the proclamation of Jesus Christ is not and cannot be a revelation of any man's election. Moreover, since the decree occurs outside of Jesus Christ—and, indeed, outside of every historical datum—Jesus himself has neither special place nor function within the totality of the decree's data, that is, within the "whatsoever comes to pass." Jesus Christ reveals no more about the nature of the decree than any other datum within it. He is no more revelatory of an individual's election than is the lily of the field. On the strict decretal view, Jesus Christ is neither the mirror of nor a window opening on the truth of an individual's election. If individual election occurs outside of Christ because God's decree itself does, Christ's position within it is like that of anything else. Hence, the proclamation of Christ does not include the proclamation of any man's own election. Only if Christ occupies the place of preeminence in the decree can he be the distinctive revelation of the nature and purpose of God's decree; and only then does election emerge as something that can be preached and believed.

We spoke of the decree as an *occurrence,* an event of God's freedom. As an event the decree has the nature of the historical. It is not an explanation of history, but the ground of the historical, rooted in the freedom of God. A decree understood as event is a created, historical truth, a product of divine freedom. Decretal theology, however, regards the decree as that which explains whatever comes to pass. Its divine decree is in fact not an *occurrence* outside of Jesus Christ: it is not an occurrence at all. Decretal theology in its purest form deifies the decree, it identifies it with God's essence and then urges that it is eternal and necessary in the same strict sense in which God himself is eternal and necessary.

If individual election is neither an occurrence inside or outside of Christ, because it is no occurrence at all, not even in God, it cannot, in the nature of the case, be preached. It can only be reduced to a principle of explanation, something to be announced only to the elect as an explanation of their Christian existence. When that happens the "religious syllogism" arises. Christians seek demonstrable "evidence" of the reality of their Christian existence. The assurance of faith is displaced by a wretched anxiety concerning the nature of one's existence before God. If election concerns the question of one's existence before God and his grace, the religious syllogism of decretal theology is of no help. Within a decree that purportedly accounts for *everything,* there can be no movement from the facts of personal repentance, faith, and love of God to assured conclusions about one's election. For the selected religious evidence is no more revelatory of the nature of God's decree in decretal thought than is one's own sin.

*   *   *

There can be no doubt that in biblical thought individuals are the object of election. Israel is an individual nation; the church is an individual social reality; Jesus was an individual whom God chose to be the Christ. Yet none of these individual realities can be defined individualistically, in terms of itself alone. Abraham is not God's elect apart from his seed; for the divine calling and election of Abraham as father of many nations depends on his seed.[3] It is in Isaac that God will elect Abraham's seed. The same is true of Jesus. His being the first-born of every creature has its reality in his church, his Body and Bride. And the same is true of the church. Its reality is unthinkable apart from Jesus' reality. Since Jesus' reality is unthinkable apart from Israel's reality, the church's reality is unthinkable apart from the reality of the nation to whom God gave the divine oracles, the covenants, the promise, the inheritance, and the gift of election.

Jesus as the Elect of God cannot be explained without Old

---

[3] The two-way interdependence of father and children, of Abraham and his seed, ultimately achieved by Christ, is expressed in the last verse of the Old Testament.

Testament Israel and the New Testament church; and Israel and the church cannot be explained apart from Jesus' reality as God's chosen Christ. The interrelationships are, however, not mutual. Jesus as the Christ is the ultimate ground of Israel and her election and of the church and its election; and Jesus is that in a sense in which neither Israel nor the church is the ultimate ground of him as the Christ. The ultimate ground of Jesus as the Christ is God's election of Jesus as the Christ, and as such Jesus is the ultimate ground of the election and reality of Israel and the church.

Individual election is *personal*. When it is defined in terms of *individualism* it is distorted. The Bible knows nothing of the election of an individual apart from the election of others. Election is the very expression of the corporate, the social, the covenantal. Election and covenant throw light on each other.

Election in biblical thought is not locked up in itself; it is open toward others, expressing the freedom of God's election and grace. This is the reason for the peculiar kind of universalism that the Bible reflects. With their individualistic definition of election as a straight line between divine decree and individual that does not even include Christ, let alone Israel or the church, decretal theologians have always been troubled by biblical language that talks about God's loving the world and Christ dying for all as a propitiation not only for our sins but for the sins of the whole world.

Individual election defined in terms of individualism is profoundly unbiblical. In biblical thought individualism bespeaks sin, death, reprobation, and hell. Individualism is an expression for separation from and opposition to God, to Christ, to one's fellow man. In theology it is a ground for Arminianism; in economics it finds expression in unbridled capitalism; in politics it works itself out as self-interest and the interest of the majority at whatever cost to whatever minority; in ethics it leads to the reduction of social ethics to personal ethics; in ecclesiology it is an argument for "free church" opposition to the worldwide catholic church confessed in the church's creeds. Individualism cannot express the Christian view of election, grace, love, covenant, cross, or resurrection; it is suited only for realities like sin, pride, death, reprobation, and hell.

*   *   *

In decretal theology the decree is single and absolutely unconditional. No part of it may be regarded as a divine response to any external condition. It absolutely determines or causes whatever comes to pass, man's fall no less than his salvation. According to its terms, God's sending his Son into the world was not a free and gracious response to man's fall into sin and death, for such a responsive reaction would mean that the decree was not a single unit but had parts and that it was conditioned by something outside of God. And that, in turn, would mean, according to decretal theology, that the decree would not be absolutely unconditional and God not absolutely sovereign.

The only modifier that can be applied to a decree that absolutely and unconditionally determines whatever comes to pass is "sovereign." The unconditional decree could not, of course, be essentially a gracious decree, since it sovereignly and unconditionally causes the fall as well as Jesus Christ, unbelief as well as faith, reprobation as well as election. The decree is both loving and hateful, blessing and curse, elective and rejective. For the Reformed language of "sovereignty of grace," scholasticism has substituted mere sovereignty. For scholastic, decretal theology, the instinctive disclosure of God's sovereignty is its determination of whatever comes to pass. Thus its character is disclosed in God's sovereign determination of the fall, and not in what God in his gracious sovereignty does to sin when he uses it to triumph over itself and to bring life out of death.

The issue is not whether God determines sin after the fall within the historical sinful situation. The Book of Acts clearly teaches that God delivered Christ to the cross with his foreknowledge and determinate counsel. The issue is rather whether God is the absolute cause of the fall, which is to say, whether God's decree involves sin as something caused by God. If so, it is not a *gracious* decree, but an ambiguous one whose nature is a mix, being essentially characterized by contraries.

Nowhere is such an ambiguous view of the divine decree taught in the Scriptures. Nowhere does the Bible indicate that God's acts of grace, mercy, compassion, and judgment are not a free divine response to the world's sinful condition. Nowhere does Scripture teach a divine reprobation not conditioned by man's sin. And nowhere do we read (as some decretal theologians, like Turretin, have said) that God sovereignly caused Adam to sin. In biblical thought the decree is a gracious decree at the heart of which stands the Christ whom God sent into the world "not to condemn the world, but that the world might be saved through him" (John 3:17).

What then is this decree of decretal theology? It is a projection of human reasoning, sometimes admittedly an inference. Support for it is often sought by appeal to human logic. Surely, it is argued, God had a plan before he began the world. He would not just begin and then "play it by ear." Even men make plans before they act. Otherwise, God's redemptive action in Christ would turn out to be no more than repair work. Surely God is not less rational than man!

But there is something fallacious about an argument that takes the human concept of plan and applies it to God, while holding all the while that God's plan has no parts and that God did nothing of the sort of thing we mean by planning, since God knows all things instantaneously. This argument for a divine plan denies the very ground from which it is launched. Nor is the pejorative use of the term "repair work" persuasive. The Bible itself, after all, regards salvation as "healing."

When they do appeal to Scripture in support of their notion of the decree, decretal theologians almost always cite three texts. One is Peter's statement in his Pentecost sermon: "this Jesus, delivered up according to the definite plan and foreknowledge of God, you crucified and killed by the hands of lawless men" (2:23). A second is from the prayer of the early church after the release of Peter and John: "for truly in this city there were gathered together against thy holy servant Jesus, whom thou didst anoint, both Herod and Pontius Pilate, with the Gentiles and the peoples of Israel, to do whatever thy hand and. thy plan had predestined to take place" (Acts 4:27, 28).

From the latter quotation, decretal theologians derive the much-used notion that God determines "whatsoever comes to pass" in his decree. They apply this notion to the whole spectrum of history, though in the passage quoted the "whatever" refers only to the crucifixion of Jesus. Decretal theologians recognize this, but they urge that if God decreed that men crucify Christ, it is legitimate to infer that God also decreed that man should fall. This is just another instance of the "in the same manner" that the Canons of Dort explicitly reject. Acts 4:27 and 28 do not teach that God decreed the fall; quite the contrary, they teach that God determined to use man's sin to overcome man's sin, and that Jews, who had the law but did not keep it, should, through lawless men (Gentiles who did not have the law), crucify Christ for the redemption and salvation of mankind.

A third passage to which decretal theologians appeal is Paul's statement to the Ephesians (1:11) that God "accomplishes all things according to the counsel of his will." The entire context argues against taking this statement to mean that God determines—and in that sense works or effectuates—"whatsoever comes to pass." Clearly, Paul does not equate "all things" with God's counsel or decree. On the contrary, he is asserting that God, according to the counsel of his will, "accomplishes all things" for the historical actualization of his purpose—the summing up in Christ of all things. God's purpose in Christ and our inheritance in it are certain, for God *accomplishes all things according to the counsel of his will.* In this entire passage Paul is speaking about God's movement in history, with its unreconciled and conflicting elements, by which he will attain his purpose.

This purposeful character of God's action gives the biblical view of history its distinctive movement toward a goal, that eschatological tendency to bring everything to its end. God's accomplishment of all things has, for the decretal theologian, no historical or eschatological dimensions, and therefore no inner reason for coming to an end. It is static and unmoving.

Paul makes very clear how God works to attain the reconciliation of all things in Christ. He points to Christ's death on the cross as that through which reconciliation is established, peace restored, and one new humanity created out of Jew and Gentile, namely, the church. The church is a visible demonstration in history of God's eternal purpose to sum up all things in Christ. Obviously, the "all things" are not themselves God's will, purpose, or good pleasure. In that kind of understanding of God's accomplishment of all things according to the plan of his will, no Christ is necessary.

Berkhof's description of God's decree is typical of how scholastic decretal theologians conceive of it:

> Reformed theology stresses the sovereignty of God in virtue of which He has sovereignly determined from all eternity whatsoever will come to pass, and works His sovereign will in His entire creation, both natural and spiritual, according to his pre-determined plan. It is in full agreement with Paul when he says that God worketh all things after the counsel of His will, Eph. 1:11. For that reason it is but natural in passing from the discussion of the Being of God to that of the works of God, it should begin with a study of the divine decrees. This is the only proper method.[4]

Note that God's decree is not defined as gracious—how could it be? The fall of man, sin, death, hell, and reprobation are not gracious determinations. Second, observe that the center of interest has shifted from the Reformation's religious and redemptive stress on the sovereignty of *grace* to a world-view that accounts for universal history in terms of mere sovereignty. Third, the decree of which Psalm 2 speaks, and the eternal purpose of God in Christ, of which Paul speaks in Ephesians, are not mentioned in this view of the decree. As a consequence, there is no inkling of recognition that it is not history as such but the goal of history that is the decreed purpose of God. Fourth, on this view, the study of the decree develops "naturally" under the study of the doctrine of God rather than (as in Calvin) under the study of the doctrine of salvation.

All of this follows from the decretal theologians' interpretation of Ephesians 1:11 as meaning that God accomplishes

---

[4] *Systematic Theology,* p. 100.

all things in such a way that whatever comes to pass reveals
the nature of his decree and his purpose.

*   *   *

In decretal theology, God's decree is a rational unity, a
concerted harmony, an eternal datum of beauty. This stems
from the singularity and simplicity of the decree. Because
God decrees and causes whatever happens, all things are seen
as a rational unity quite apart from Christ's *reconciliation* of
everything. The Bible presents a quite different view. It
teaches that God works in, through, by means of, and against
the data of history, and that Christ works in history to sum
up and reconcile what is opposed to the gracious purpose of
the divine will. In the biblical statement of God's purpose,
history is the turbulent and bloodied arena in which, for all
its opposition to God, God sovereignly moves to achieve his
gracious purpose.

Scripture presents God as one who wars against evil and
evil men and utters his judgment to accomplish salvation.
Psalm 76 declares that in Judah God is known, and in Israel
his name is great because he breaks the arrows, the shield, the
sword, and the weapons of war. He is a God to be feared, for
he pronounces his judgment from heaven to save the oppressed of the earth. In praise of such a God the psalmist
declares (vs. 10): "Surely the wrath of men shall praise thee;
the residue of wrath thou wilt gird upon thee." If everything
that happens expresses God's sovereign will, what meaning
can be given to statements such as these about God's sentence of judgment, his anger, and his use and restraint of the
wrath of men? If indeed God restrains what he himself wills,
he would be working counter to himself. Decretal theologians
must, therefore, simply ignore these biblical descriptions of
God's historical actions and reactions to human history, or
strip them of theological significance by asserting that they
are apparent contradictions or mere anthropomorphisms.

The Bible plainly teaches that God determines that the sins
of men will serve God's redemptive purposes. God determined that sinful men would crucify Christ and thereby

contribute to the achievement of God's redemptive purpose. God indeed uses sin for his saving purpose. It belongs to the very essence of the good news that God can and will bring light out of darkness, possibility out of impossibility, good out of evil, life out of death, resurrection out of crucifixion. The God of the Bible can call the things that are not as though they were; he can bring Isaac out of a barren woman and fatherhood out of a man too old to be a father; he can call and create the nation of Israel out of nothing; he can bring forth the Christ out of a virgin; he can reconcile all things separated, hostile, inimical to each other. He can give life to a valley of dead bones.

The whole story of the Bible is the story of a God who speaks with a power both sovereign and gracious, in creation and in redemption, a God who brings order out of chaos, good out of evil, and eternal life out of the death of his own Son. The resurrection happens not on some extra-historical plane, but in and from the realm of death (see Rom. 1:4). It is in the grave that God fashions life, out of darkness that he causes light to shine forth.

God turns sin against itself and makes it the instrument of man's salvation. It is by death that God overcomes death, by sin that God overcomes sin (see Heb. 2:14). In his gracious plan the purposes of sin and death are turned against themselves, for within their realities and against their purposed intent, God sovereignly achieves his gracious purpose in Christ, the triumph of life and righteousness. We have also seen the truth of this reflected in God's turning the sin and unbelief of Israel into the salvation of the Gentiles. Unbelieving Jews are the enemies of the gospel for the sake of the Gentiles. Out of Jewish hostility, God works the salvation of Gentiles.

Here lies the miracle, the mystery, of redemption! Death is defeated—not far from it, not alongside of it, but *within* and *through* it. Sin is overcome through sin. Gentile salvation is fashioned out of Jewish animosity to the gospel. In this the sovereign—and, no less, gracious—power of God is disclosed. If the church is to understand itself, it must recognize this, for its very existence derives from God's deployment of

Israel's unbelief. This is the nature of the good news, which the very existence of the church reflects.

*   *   *

The Reformed scholastic view of God's decree is burdened with extraordinary religious difficulties, as we have seen throughout this study. The understanding of God as exhaustively rational theoretically deprives him of his freedom. The identification of God's decree with his essence (or with his will defined in terms of his essence) deifies the decree and makes the decree eternal and simple in the sense in which eternality and simplicity belong to God only. The simplification of the decree makes it unknowable to the human mind. The eternalization of the decree leads decretal theology to lose its grasp on all created and historical reality. The deification of the decree theoretically excludes the possibility, on one hand, of any authentic movement of God out of himself in an act of creation, and, on the other, of any authentic personal relationship of God to the world. And the deification of the decree is the matrix of its rejection of the conditionality that expresses God's freedom (something quite other than the Arminian notion of conditionality).

All of this compels decretal theology to redefine God's grace, mercy, compassion, and patience in a peculiar way that regards God as being all these things to himself. Finally, the decree of decretal theology is internally closed to history and to the eschatological, to the emergence of what Turretin called an "addition," but what in biblical idiom is the new, the good news—good because it is *gracious* and news because it is something new wrought by the freedom of God. All these threats to the gospel can be avoided by remaining within the biblical boundaries and eschewing the rationalistic temptation to infer things from biblical teachings that violate the content of Scripture.

Decretal theology defines God's decree as that which accounts for every eventuation. But what is the biblical concept of God's decree? The term decree, meaning an exact and determined enactment, is used only in the Old Testament, always in reference to nature—with one exception. In Psalm

2:7 it is used in reference to the election of the messiah-king—an immediate reference to a king of Israel, and an ultimate reference to Jesus Christ, the son of David who will sit on David's throne forever.

This use of "decree" to refer to election in Psalm 2 is cited in the New Testament. The early church harked back to it in prayer and praise in reference to Jesus Christ (Acts 4:25, 27). In the same passage reference is made to the crucifixion of Christ by Herod and Pontius Pilate, who, with the Gentiles and the people of Israel, were gathered "to do whatever thy hand and thy plan had predestined to take place" (vs. 28). The idea of decree in biblical usage relates specifically to Jesus and his election by God. In Acts 4 God's decree and plan relate specifically to the crucifixion and crucifiers of Christ. In this event of crucifixion, *in this city* (vs. 27), the decree of God is centered; and at this center its truth and meaning are revealed. Decretal theology overlooks this, in favor of a view of the worldwide expanse of history with God's decree defined in terms of "whatsoever comes to pass."

Decretal theology's eye for the universal reference, for "whatsoever comes to pass," prevents it from looking at any event in particular. It pays no special attention to what Psalm 2 asserts when it declares "I will tell of the decree," nor to Paul's words concerning God's eternal purpose in Christ to reconcile all things. In defining God's decree decretal theology neither looks at any particular event, nor at all events. How could it? Many have not yet happened. Decretal theology's "whatsoever comes to pass" is, in short, abstract principle. In sharp contrast, the Bible fixes our attention on a single event—the event of Jesus Christ—and from this single point looks at all of human history. In Scripture, God's decree is revealed in Jesus Christ.

Why do the nations conspire? the psalmist asks. Why do their rulers consult together against Yahweh and his anointed? God laughs at such puny opposition, for he has set his messiah-king on the holy hill of Zion. The final form of this messiah-king, we have noted, is Christ himself. This messiah-king says: "I will tell of the decree of the Lord: He said to me, 'You are my Son; today I have begotten you.' "

Here in the language and form of the Old Testament, Christ is declaring that he will tell us about the nature and content of God's decree. This is it: Yahweh told me that I, the Christ, am God's anointed Son, God's Messiah, God's Elect. And Yahweh explained this by adding, "Today I have begotten you." Christ is God's Elect not by virtue of God's eternal generation nor by virtue of an eternal necessity rooted in God's necessary and eternal essence, but by virtue of *today,* the day of God's freedom in which God freely begat Jesus. The "today" of Psalm 2 talks about the freedom of God, the historicity of the divine decree in which God elected and created Jesus to be Christ.

The divine decree of Psalm 2, which both creates and elects what it creates is no less universal than the decree of decretal theology. The decree of decretal theology covers everything. The decree of God of which the messiah-king speaks in Psalm 2 also covers everything. But the movement of thought is vastly different. Decretal theology begins with "whatsoever comes to pass"; biblical thought begins with one event, Jesus Christ, and from this center looks out on all of world history. In telling about God's decree, the messiah-king reports that God said: "Ask of me, and I will make the nations your heritage, and the ends of the earth your possession." This covers whatever is contained in all time and space, no less than does the decree of decretal theology.

But there is a profound difference. The decree of decretal theology can be announced, but not preached, for preaching is an appeal to a condition and thus a violation of unconditionality. Decretal theology's eternal decree lacks the "today," a day that bespeaks both the freedom of God, and the unique significance of that event of the "today" of freedom in which God freely—not by the implication of his essence— brought forth Jesus as the Christ, his chosen.

Because the decree of Psalm 2 is wrought in divine freedom, and is thus historical and contingent, an event of "today," Psalm 2 can conclude with an appeal. While the decree of decretal theology can be announced or apologetically asserted, the decree of God as defined in Psalm 2 can be preached in the authentic biblical understanding of preaching. Psalm 2 concludes with a sermonic appeal: "Now therefore, O kings, be wise; be warned, O rulers of the earth. Serve the Lord with fear, with trembling kiss his feet, lest he be angry and you perish in the way."

Similarly decretal theology gives no special attention to Paul's assertion that God's eternal purpose is what he realized in Jesus Christ (Eph. 3:11). Just as it defines election in isolation from Paul's teaching that it occurs in Christ (Eph. 1:4), it defines God's decree without allowing Paul's teaching that God's purpose is realized in Christ to enter in. This is no accident. A doctrine of election that occurs in Christ and a divine decree that is by its very nature God's decreed purpose in Christ, are an election and a decree that are not only eternal but also historical. But decretal theology, operating only with the concept of God's necessary and eternal essence and defining the decree in terms of this concept, prohibits itself from taking seriously the elective decree as a divine event occurring in Christ. It cannot do so because it insists that God's decree (in which election is only one factor) of "whatsoever comes to pass" *cannot regard the decree as itself something that comes to pass.* What explains all of history cannot itself be historical. With this, the problem of Lessing returns.

The truth and meaning of election and of the divine decree lie in Jesus Christ, for Christ in biblical thought is God's election and God's decree. The truth of divine election and of God's decree is revealed in Christ, for both occur in Christ. As the event of God's election and decree, Christ is not merely the one who reveals an abstract election and decree that occurs outside of him. Christ is no mere medium through which an eternal truth of election and decree is announced. This is the error of all forms of Christian rationalism. In the language (though not the meaning) of McLuhan, Christ is the medium who is also the message. Christ reveals the truth about God's election and decree because he himself is the truth and reality of God's decree.[5] When Paul describes the purpose and grace of God, he speaks of these as given in

---

[5] Mention the word Calvinism (or the Reformed faith) and most Christians, and even many non-Christians, immediately think of election. If only this meant God's election of Jesus Christ! Then at least men would know, as did the Jews at

and revealed through Christ. He writes to Timothy about the God "who saved us . . . in virtue of his own purpose and the grace which he gave us in Christ Jesus ages ago, and now has manifested through the appearing of our Savior Christ Jesus" (II Tim. 1:9, 10).

In revealing and proclaiming God's election and decree, Christ proclaims himself. He did so, Luke says, in his first sermon (4:16-30) in Nazareth. The claim he made then was what finally provoked his crucifixion and the mockery of those standing around his cross. On Pentecost Peter proclaimed God's election in terms of Jesus, and God's decree in that concrete form in which men, Jews and Gentiles, crucified Christ according to God's decree in order that through this event of rejection and crucifixion God might make Jesus both Lord and Christ. When Saul understands this he becomes the Paul who can proclaim Jesus as God's Elect and regard him as God's chosen Christ, the one in whom God's eternal purpose resides.

When Paul understood Jesus as God's Elect and *as such* the embodiment of God's eternal purpose, he not only accepted Christ but proclaimed him—not only to the chosen nation (the church) (that is, "in due time and place") but to the whole world of the Gentiles. Once Paul understood the truth of God's election and the nature of God's elective, gracious decree as disclosed in Jesus Christ, "the chosen of God," Paul could preach the gospel of God's election and decree to any and all men, Jew or Gentile.

*   *   *

Suppose that God does not have the kind of plan envisioned by decretal theology? Suppose this decree is only the hypostatized image of human rationality imposed on God by a presumptuous scholasticism eager to explain everything? Suppose that it is improper to postulate a divine plan constructed in terms of the simplicity and rationality of God's

the cross, what the issue really is, and if they rejected it, they would know what they were rejecting. But the pulpit has allowed—with repeated assists from theology—election to become caricatured. Many who reject election have only rejected a caricature of it.

essence? Suppose that it is unwarranted to attribute deity
and divine eternality to such a plan?

What would be lost if such a decree were abandoned?
Every essential feature of it is humanly unknowable. A decree without distinctions is by that fact not an object of
human knowledge. Decretal theologians themselves admit
that we can know the simplicity of the divine decree only in
terms of multiplicity. So the assertion that God's decree is as
uncompounded as God himself means literally nothing. What
can it mean to assert that individual election stems from a
decree that itself contains no such distinction?

Furthermore, the deification of the decree achieved by
grounding it in God's essence and attributing the divine
qualities of simplicity and eternity to it asserts that the
decree is in effect God. Within that assertion, it is meaningless to assert that God *has* a plan. If the decree is not an
"addition" to God, it truly *is* God. But one does not say that
God *has* what he *is*. God is love, for example, but the
meaning of this statement is not expressed by saying that
God *has* love.

Again, suppose we reject the position that God is the
ultimate cause and source of sin (as most Reformed theologians do). What is left of the meaning of this all-comprehensive decree of God? Without the principle of the divine
causality of sin, the decree of decretal theology is empty and
meaningless. Since sin pervades all reality, an all-comprehensive decree that determines whatever comes to pass *must*
retain the divine causality of sin if it is to retain any meaning
at all.

What is left of decretal theology's sin-determinative decree
if its determination of sin is removed? Its distinctive feature
would indeed be lost. What is secondary—by its standards—
would remain. But what is by its standards secondary is by
biblical standards primary—God's saving determination in and
through Christ to employ sin against itself in order to triumph over it. Decretal theologians will object that such a
decree is quite unlike the traditional decree of decretal theology. But the decree that triumphs over sin is quite like the
one Paul discusses in Ephesians—God's eternal purpose which
he has realized in Christ Jesus our Lord (3:11). The disregard

that decretal theologians have shown for this Pauline teaching
stems from their theological methodology—the fact that they
place the decree within their doctrine of God, in which Jesus
plays no role.

*   *   *

Decretal theologians admit that the decree is not described
in the abstract in Scripture, but is rather set in its historical
realization. If they took this seriously, they would recognize
that the actualization of God's decree in history is also the
revelation of the nature of the decree. And in loyalty to the
revelation of God's decree one ought to seek the nature of
the decree within its historical disclosure rather than deciding
in terms of one's own understanding of God's nature, what
such a decree must be! Decretal theologians reason that since
God is simple, the decree must be simple, and so forth. But if
the decree must conform thus to God's nature, why not its
actualization as well? Naturally, if its actualization conformed to God's nature, the created universe would also be
divine and without parts or moments.

Would it not be better to take more seriously the biblical
record of the revelation and actualization of the divine decree? Such an approach would not provide an *a priori* principle for interpreting universal history, but it does furnish a
luminous insight into the nature and reality of the Lord Jesus
Christ.

In deference to the decretal tradition Berkhof, for example, admits that Scripture speaks of the decree only in the
concrete forms of the historical, but then immediately turns
away from the Bible to the Westminster Shorter Catechism
and defines the decree in the abstract terms of an eternal
foreordination of whatever comes to pass. He derives the
decree from God as he necessarily is in himself and then—
apart from its actualization and revelation in history as described in Scripture, and without reference to Christ—defines
the decree as it is in itself. The actual historical revelation of
the decree as recorded in Scripture is disregarded as nondefin-
itive.

It may seem strange that a conservative and biblically oriented theologian like Berkhof would define the decree abstractly in the face of its biblical presentation. But it must be recalled that it is axiomatic for decretal theologians that the historical is not an ingredient of the decree defined wholly in terms of God as he is in himself. Decretal theologians are not likely to offer many prooftexts to indicate that their decree has biblical sanction; in fact, they seek their sanction by arguing that nothing has meaning except on the basis of such a view or by asserting that such a view is sustained not so much by particular texts as by the whole fabric of the Bible. If such appeals seem odd, recall that the decree of these theologians, which purports to explain all history, is not itself explained by history. Thus no biblical text can prove the decree, since every biblical text is itself a historical datum. What explains all of history cannot employ history as explanation. Within the terms of an abstract decree, the best the decretal theologian can do is a philosophical appeal to meaningfulness or a vague theological appeal to the general character of Scripture. A decree that accounts for history, but in which the dimension of the historical is not an ingredient, cannot appeal to history, not even to biblical history (that is, a biblical teaching or text) to establish its validity.

Since this decree is said to account for everything that comes to pass, it cannot account for anything authentically historical. If every item of history is decreed, the very possibility of the historical is excluded. All things cannot work together for good, because they already *are*, as willed by God, good. Moreover, if each event is God's decreed will, history is excluded, for no single event is historical. The historical requires movement between one reality and another, one event and another. There is nothing within decretal theology's decree that can allow for historical movement.

Why not take seriously Berkhof's observation that the divine decree confronts us in Scripture in its historical concreteness? This would liberate us from an ahistorical decree, and free us to recognize a goal-oriented decree, working in and through history on all things to achieve God's eternal

purpose. We could then give its due to that concrete purpose
of God which he realized in Christ. Fleeing abstractions, we
could see that all the historically concrete Old and New
Testament terms to which Berkhof refers—God's will, counsel, purpose, good pleasure, wisdom—are in biblical thought
associated with Christ, and are for that reason not at all
abstract. As the one in whom God delights as in no other,
Christ, God's Elect, is the mystery of God's will and the
reality of his eternal purpose.

In the light of all this, why do we need to look for another
decree, one purposed outside of Christ, one unknowable to
us because of a divine simplicity, one unrelated to history?
By what right and for what purpose should we settle for a
decree outside of Christ that so reduces all things to equal
significance that Christ is no more than one event among
whatever comes to pass, willed by God equally and in the
same manner as the fall? Is not such a decree the ultimate
expression of a rationalism seeking the intellectual mastery
necessary to make all things transparently reasonable to the
human mind?

Decretal theologians may admit that the absolute rationality of all things is exhaustively transparent only to God, and
that man's knowledge of this rationality is, though real,
analogical. But the real test is in the religious arena. No
Christian would say that God's grace as displayed on the
cross is irrational; what Christian would dare say that Christ's
death for him was an act of rationality and nothing more?
Would not every Christian urge that grace is more than
rational, and that God's forgiveness of sins is not wholly
explicable in terms of rationality? What Christian would
stand before the God who gives him grace and declare to God
that his bestowal of grace and forgiveness is a wholly and
only reasonable thing for God to do?

When we stand before the decree of God as realized and
revealed in Jesus Christ, all attempts to rationalize our own
reception of grace—or indeed the unbelief of anyone else—are
excluded as inappropriate invasions of the holy. We do not
urge that our reception of grace stands to reason. The human
mind will never rationally understand why God loves us as he

does in Christ. It can only be overwhelmed with the wonder of God's grace.

*   *   *

We must now look more closely at how our election is involved in the election of Christ. According to Paul, we are elected in Christ (Eph. 1:4) and are God's "workmanship, created in Christ Jesus" (Eph. 2:10). Again we see the correlation of election and creation. The Christian is what he is by virtue of his divine election and creation in Christ. This correlation of election and creation is grounded in the correlation of election and creation that constitutes the reality of Jesus as the Christ. The baby of Bethlehem, Jesus of Nazareth, is both God's creation (in the language of Psalm 2 the one whom God has begotten) and the elect of God, the one whom God by his election made to be both Lord and Christ (Acts 2:36). Our existence and reality as Christians are constituted by our election and creation by God in Christ, whose own reality is in turn constituted by his election and creation by God. From this it is clear that in biblical thought the divine elective and creative action that constitutes our reality as Christians is not merely grounded in, but is constituted by, that divine elective and creative action which constitutes the reality of Jesus as the chosen of God. Therefore the election of the Christian is inextricably bound up with the election of Christ. Though the interrelationship between the two is not one of mutuality ("in the same manner"), it is such that the election of the Christian is only definable in terms of God's election of Christ.

The Heidelberg Catechism is most interesting on this point. Question 29 asks "Why is the Son of God called *Jesus,* that is, *Savior?*" The nontheoretical, wholly practical, religious answer is that he, and none other, saves us. The Catechism then moves to the larger question, "Why is He called *Christ,* that is, *Anointed?*" (Q. 31). The answer is "Because he is ordained [chosen] of God the Father, and anointed with the Holy Spirit, to be our chief Prophet and Teacher, who has fully revealed to us the secret counsel and will of God

concerning our redemption; and our only High Priest . . . and
our eternal King."

Observe that Jesus the Son of God is said to be the Christ
because he was ordained, that is, elected, by God and therefore anointed with the Spirit. By virtue of this divine election
and anointing Jesus, the Son of God, is said to reveal fully
"the secret counsel and will of God concerning our redemption." If that is true, what remains of that position of
decretal theology that all our knowledge of God's decree
must appear to us as contradictory to human rationality? But
the first observation is even more interesting in the light of
the next question. The Catechism goes on to ask "But why
are you called a Christian?" The answer: "Because I am a
member of Christ by faith, and thus a partaker of His
anointing. . . ."

Let us first consider the question. It is an expression of
amazement. Since there is only one Christ—the Son of God—
and "no salvation is to be sought or found in any other,"
why do believers in Christ bear his name as a designation of
what they are? In biblical thought a person's name indicates
what he *is*. No Christian is the Christ. Yet every Christian
identifies himself, and is willing to be known to others, by
reference to the name of Christ. Why does a Christian who
acknowledges that there is only one Christ risk confusing
matters by himself bearing the name of Christ?

The Catechism answers this by declaring that the believer
is "a member of Christ by faith, and thus a partaker of his
anointing" and, therefore, shares in Christ's threefold office.
While it is not explicitly asserted that the Christian participates
in Christ's ordination or election by God, the Christian is
said to partake of Christ's anointing. Since "Anointed" is the
meaning of the word Christ, and since the question asked is
why believers bear the name of Christ, the idea that the
believer shares in the election of Christ is plain even though it
is not explicit.

Jesus is the Christ because of his election. If the believer
bears—in the profound, biblical sense—the name of Christ by
bearing the name of Christian, he does so because he shares in
the election of Christ. The idea that we share or participate in
Christ is characteristic of the Christian religion. We share in

Christ's death, his resurrection, his Spirit, his ascension, his return, his judgment of the world, his threefold task as prophet, priest, and king, his suffering, his kingdom, power, and glory. And we share in his election. That we do so is only another expression for the fact that election in biblical thought is never a purely individual matter. The election of the believer, as that of Israel and the church, is an involvement in the divine election of Jesus.

Election is not the one point at which the Bible goes individualistic. Yet almost every great doctrinal controversy in Reformed theology has arisen from the individualistic character of its doctrine of election. In biblical thought the believer shares in all that Christ is and does. Christ is the only Son of God, yet the Bible says that we are sons of God; his death is unique, yet we are said to have died with him; Jesus is the only Christ and all others are false, yet believers bear his name. This truth is also echoed in the Heidelberg Catechism. Believers are said to be ingrafted into Christ and to receive all his benefits (Q. 20) and to be "partakers of Him and of all His treasures and gifts" (Q. 55). One of Christ's benefits is his election by God, which makes him preeminent in all things. As these words assert—and as the Lord's Supper celebrates—believers are partakers of *him*. This is the mystery of eating his body and drinking his blood. To partake of Christ is to partake also of the election that constitutes him as the Christ.[6]

The idea of participation in Christ's election spells the end of any purely individualistic doctrine of election and the illegitimacy of theologically tailoring the gospel to fit such a doctrine. It liberates us from the insoluble problem that a merely individual election raises for the proclamation of the gospel. It makes election the language of grace, thereby removing its vulnerability to rational manipulation in terms of logical inferences and implications.

6 No concept seems better to reflect the manner in which the national election of Israel relates to the election of Christ than the concept of participation. The same holds true, it would seem, for the church. If the church does not *participate* in (partake of and live by) Christ's election, it is the only aspect of Christ in which the church does not share. But in that case how could Paul declare that the church is the "fulness of Christ"?

The truth of election as participation in Christ's election can be spoken only in the idiom of faith and worship, in the language of proclamation that summons men to believe. This means that the truth of election is not a biblical base from which reprobation can be projected as a biblical explanation of the fact that some men do not believe. For Christ is the truth of election, the reason that some men are saved, *but not the reason that some are not.* This means that any doctrine of reprobation is illegitimate by biblical standards *except that which biblical teaching sanctions:* that he who rejects God, God rejects. Any doctrine of reprobation that goes beyond the biblical teaching of election, any doctrine of reprobation that arises outside of faith by the power of human logic, must be regarded as biblically indefensible.

The truth of election, as biblically taught, accounts in terms of grace for the election of Israel, of Christ, and of the church, and, within these boundaries, for the election of an individual; but it does not thereby posit a basis on which, in the name of reason and logic, a rejected counterpart to Israel, to Christ, and to the church may be projected. The gracious elective and creative act of God that accounts for the reality of Israel, Christ, and the church has no corresponding negative power that posits a reprobative counterpart to these realities, as the rationalistic interpretation maintains. Election, as an act of grace, is so unique and incomparable that it has no counterpart, *not even a negative reprobative counterpart.* Election no more logically implies and necessitates reprobation, than the existence of God logically implies and necessitates the devil. Reprobation defined as the logical implicate of election is an expression of a dualistic view of reality: if there is a God there must also be a devil; if there is a Christ there must also be antichrist; if there are elect there must also be reprobate; if there is good there must also be evil; if there is a redeemed church there must also be an unredeemed and damned world; if God sent Christ to save the world he must also have sent Christ to damn the world.

Grace has a redemptive bias. Logic has no bias. It is neutral about all things, heartless, ignorant of grace, mercy and compassion for sinners. The whole biblical message is a rejection of this view. Nothing in the Bible suggests that God created the world to save some men and damn others. Nothing in the Bible suggests that God elected Israel in order to damn all Gentile nations. Nothing in the Bible suggests that God sent Christ into the world both to save and damn. On this matter the Apostle is unequivocal: "God sent the Son into the world *not to condemn the world,* but that the world might be saved through him."

*   *   *

If it were recognized that there is only one election, one saving decree of God, centered and embodied in Christ and related to Israel and the church in the same manner as Christ is related to Israel and the church and both of these to Christ, it should be clear that election can, indeed *must,* be preached. To preach Christ is to preach election; and to preach election is to preach Christ. To preach election will then be as easy and as difficult, but no easier and no more difficult, than to preach Christ as the ground and fulfilment of the meaning of Israel and as the fulness of the church. For this is what Christ *is:* the fulfilment of Israel and the fulness of the church. He himself proclaimed the former in his first sermon in Nazareth when he read from Isaiah, sat down and declared: "Today this scripture has been fulfilled in your hearing" (Luke 4:21). And Paul declared the latter when he referred to the church as "his body, the fulness of him who fills all in all" (Eph. 1:23).

Let the church preach election, and let it center its proclamation of election on God's election of Jesus to be the Christ. Let it show how Christ's election is related to the election of Israel and of the church. Let it proclaim that to believe on Jesus as the Christ is to believe in his election, and in this belief to discover that one shares in Christ's election as one also in faith discovers that he shares in Christ's death and resurrection and, indeed, in Christ's past and unending future.

Failure to preach Jesus as the chosen of God tends to obscure a great deal of truth about Jesus. To be sure, the concept of election is contained in the concept "Christ" ("Anointed"), so that any preaching of Jesus as the Christ

implicitly proclaims the election of Jesus. Yet I am afraid that
most people, both in and outside the church, regard the title
"Christ" as either synonymous with the name "Jesus," or as
merely a kind of second name. Ignorance of the election of
Jesus seems characteristic of many revivalist movements, including the contemporary Jesus movement. What is ignored is
that the affirmation that Jesus is the Christ, the chosen of
God, is the most distinctively religious thing that can be said
about him. The earliest Christian confession was that Jesus is
the Christ. The early believers were not called Jesus People
but Christians—and that by nonbelievers who recognized that
Jesus was preached *as the Christ* by the church. The topic of
Jesus' first sermon, the topic of Peter's proclamation on
Pentecost, the theme of Paul, the apostle to the Gentiles, and
the central issue at the cross was that Jesus is not really
known or believed unless he is known and believed as the
Christ, "the chosen of God."

*   *   *

At Miletus, en route to Jerusalem for the last time, Paul
called together the elders of the church of Ephesus. During
his meeting with them, he said, "I did not shrink from
declaring to you the whole counsel of God" (Acts 20:27).
Decretal theologians often quote this text to urge the necessity of preaching "the whole counsel of God." But what they
mean by this is ambiguous. Since they define the counsel of
God as whatever comes to pass, to preach the whole counsel
would mean to preach everything that comes to pass. But this
is impossible, for all things have not yet come to pass, and
even if it were possible, such preaching would hardly reflect
Paul's determination to preach nothing but Jesus Christ and
him crucified. What decretal theologians seem to mean is that
the church ought to proclaim that God determines whatever
comes to pass. But this single datum of divine determinism
bears no recognizable relationship to what actually is the
whole counsel of God. If the whole counsel of God is simply
the truth that God determines whatever comes to pass, the
whole counsel of God is simply a principle of determination
that could have been preached before the fall. This is some-

thing quite different from the good news of what God in
grace has done through Jesus Christ about man's sin. Paul did
not preach whatever happens, nor did he preach that whatever happens is determined by God. Paul preached the whole
counsel of God in that eternal purpose which God realized in
Christ, the defeat and reduction to nought of sin and death.

When God's purpose as biblically defined is achieved, God
terminates history. If history in itself were what God decrees,
then the end (termination) of history would also be the end
(termination) of God's purportedly eternal decree. What God
has decreed is neither history defined as "whatsoever comes to
pass," nor history as something that (like life) merely ends.
The decree fulfilled is the goal of history, and as fulfilled the
decree does not end but eternally abides. As God's creation
of the world moves toward a *Sabbath,* God moves in sinful
history toward a triumph over history that ends, not in a
mere termination, but in an *eternal* Sabbath, because nothing
remains to be done, the divine purpose having been fulfilled.
According to Paul, God triumphs over sinful history by using
sinful history for its own defeat and for the triumph of God's
gracious purpose in Christ. And this purpose is the reconciliation and unification of all broken, fragmented, unreconciled
and hostile things, whether in heaven or on earth, in Christ,
so that Christ attains this preeminence over all things because
he reconciles all things. Such a decree can be preached, for it
is not exhausted in time by merely coming to pass. It can be
preached, for it is the eternal truth of the gospel.

Decretal theology cannot accept such a divine decree because it does not derive from God's necessary being and
essence, but from his freedom to respond to the human
condition of sin and death. Commitment to the decree of
decretal theology, however, exacts its toll: God loses that
freedom, Christ is deprived of his preeminence in the decreed
purpose of God, and the gospel is so restrictively defined that
the church is no longer free to preach it as good news to "all
nations and every creature."

The biblical witness safeguards the freedom of God's gracious actions toward and in the world. It preserves the truth
that grace is unmerited and that election is not man's choice
of God. That God's decree is said to be before the creation of

the world does not mean that time and space are merely a
stage on which God acts out his decree. If they were, God's
actions in time (as history) would be mere theater. Time and
space as God's creation are themselves a part of the decree.
They are the forms in which God willed to be with man.

Time and space, as history itself, have their ultimate meaning in Jesus Christ, which is to say, in the freedom of God.
Every attempt to understand such biblical expressions as
"from before the foundation of the world" in terms of "time
before time," of "history before history" (which is to say in
terms of a decree of *deified eternality and activity*), ignores
both the freedom of God and the historical character of a
decree wrought in this freedom. Precisely because the dimensions of time, space, and history characterize the divine
decree, its actualization and revelation can only be known
within these dimensions. The clue to the secret of the decree
does not lie in something behind it, nor in time and space
understood as dimensions extrinsic to it.

Biblical thought excludes a definition of eternity by a
backward projection of time. Since time is a concomitant of
creation, time may not be posited prior to creation. God's
decree, therefore, may not be defined in terms of a projection of antecedent time, nor in terms of the necessary eternality of the divine being.

In religious language, "Jesus Christ" says it all. He is the
revelation of God's grace and election, of God's freedom to
create, to respond to and become involved in the world
without ceasing to be the eternal God. The Father of our
Lord Jesus Christ can, in his freedom, involve himself in
creation, even in a fallen, death-ridden world, "for us men
and for our salvation." Jesus Christ is the proof. Jesus Christ,
therefore, is the "mirror of election," the clue to the nature
of our election, which God decreed in him. The Son tells us
of God's decree when he tells us what Yahweh (the name of
the God who in freedom covenanted with man) told him
(what more explicit disclosure of the decree could there be?),
namely, "You are my Son, today I have begotten you." Here
we are told that the very existence of Christ, the Anointed
and Elect of God, constitutes Christ as himself the decree.
Christ is God's decree by virtue of the fact that he is "begot-

ten" of God. God made him to be the Christ. The Christ is begotten of God, not in the "day" of God's own necessary eternality, but "today," the day of God's freedom, the day that might never have been!

In Christ, therefore, lies the fulness of the reality and meaning of God's decree, a fulness only known to faith. In him, therefore, lies the reality and meaning of our personal election, together with that of Israel and the church. As Calvin said, "But if we have been chosen in Him, we shall not find assurance of our election in ourselves; and not even in God the Father, if we conceive of him as severed from his Son." The assurance of election can only be found where election is and occurs, namely, in Jesus Christ, who owes his existence and his election to that particular and distinctive day of God's freedom on which God begat him and thereby made him both Lord and Christ. And assurance of our election and true knowledge of the whole biblical truth about election will never be found if we place a gap between Father and Son and insert into this gap a decree, defined wholly in terms of the Father, in which Jesus Christ has no more status than anything else that comes to pass.

Index

207